INTRO

Logic

THIS
SENTENCE
IS A LIE.

Dan Cryan, Sharron Shatil and Bill Mayblin

Edited by Richard Appignanesi

ICON BOOKS UK   TOTEM BOOKS USA

Published in the UK in 2001
by Icon Books Ltd., Grange Road,
Duxford, Cambridge CB2 4QF
E-mail: info@iconbooks.co.uk
www.iconbooks.co.uk

Published in the USA in 2002
by Totem Books
Inquiries to: Icon Books Ltd.,
Grange Road, Duxford,
Cambridge CB2 4QF, UK

Sold in the UK, Europe, South Africa
and Asia by Faber and Faber Ltd.,
3 Queen Square, London WC1N 3AU
or their agents

Distributed to the trade in the USA by
National Book Network Inc.,
4720 Boston Way, Lanham,
Maryland 20706

Distributed in the UK, Europe,
South Africa and Asia by
Macmillan Distribution Ltd.,
Houndmills, Basingstoke RG21 6XS

Distributed in Canada by
Penguin Books Canada,
10 Alcorn Avenue, Suite 300,
Toronto, Ontario M4V 3B2

Published in Australia in 2001
by Allen & Unwin Pty. Ltd.,
PO Box 8500, 83 Alexander Street,
Crows Nest, NSW 2065

ISBN 1 84046 345 7

Printed and bound in Australia
by McPherson's Printing Group, Victoria

What is Logic?

Nothing is more natural to conversation than argument. We try to convince the person we are arguing with that we are right, that our conclusion follows from something that they will accept. It would be no good if we could not tell when one thing followed from another. What is often passed off in conversation as an argument does not fit the bill.

This is clearly rubbish because there is nothing to link the truth of the conclusion to the truth of the supporting claims. What we need is to ensure that the truth of the supporting claims is preserved by the argument. Logic is quite simply the study of *truth-preserving arguments*.

Studying Sentences

The Greek philosopher **Aristotle** (384–322 BC) first gave us the idea of a tool (*organon*) to argue convincingly. This study included grammar, rhetoric and a theory of interpretation, as well as logic. The first thing Aristotle does is discuss sentences.

SENTENCES COME IN THREE TYPES ...

1. Singular:	Socrates is a man.
2. Universal:	Every man is mortal.
3. Particular:	Some men are mortal.

IN EACH OF THESE TYPES WE ARE SAYING THAT SOMETHING OR SOME THINGS ARE OF A CERTAIN KIND.

The objects we talk about (e.g., nouns like *Socrates* and *tables*; abstract nouns like *walking*; and pronouns like *someone* and *everyone*) Aristotle calls the **subject** of the sentence.

What we say about the subject of the sentence (e.g., verbs like *is eating* and *has fallen*; adjectives like *is difficult*; and nouns like *man* in things like "Socrates is a man") Aristotle called the **predicate**.

The Square of Oppositions

Aristotle noticed that the truth of some subject-predicate sentences has an effect on the truth of other subject-predicate sentences.

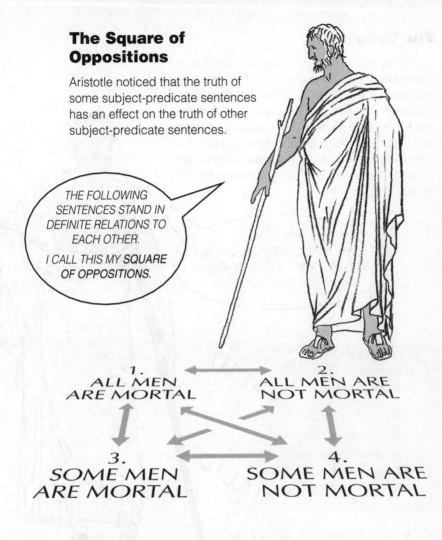

THE FOLLOWING SENTENCES STAND IN DEFINITE RELATIONS TO EACH OTHER.

I CALL THIS MY SQUARE OF OPPOSITIONS.

1.
ALL MEN ARE MORTAL

2.
ALL MEN ARE NOT MORTAL

3.
SOME MEN ARE MORTAL

4.
SOME MEN ARE NOT MORTAL

Sentences **1** and **2** cannot both be true.

The diagonal statements **1** and **4** are known as **contradictories**. As long as there are men, one of them has to be true but never both – the truth of one guarantees that the other is false.

The same is true for diagonal statements **2** and **3**.

Sentences **1** and **3** cannot both be false but can both be true. If **1** is true then so is **3**, but not the other way around.

Similarly with **2** and **4**. The same relation holds between "**All men are mortal**" and "**Socrates is mortal**".

The Syllogism

Using the square of oppositions, Aristotle noticed a mysterious fact. Take a sentence like "Socrates is a man". If an argument of three statements is built where the subject of the first statement is the predicate of the second (call these the **premises**) and the third statement is composed of the remaining terms (call this the **conclusion**), then the truth of the conclusion is guaranteed by the truth of the premises.

> THIS SCHEMA I CALL A **SYLLOGISM**. WE CAN USE IT TO SEE WHY ONE ARGUMENT IS TRUE AND ANOTHER FALSE.

1. All men are mortal.
2. Socrates is a man.
3. Socrates is mortal.

VALID

1. All carnivores eat meat.
2. Some birds are not carnivores.
3. Some birds don't eat meat.

VALID

1. I support Arsenal.
2. Bergkamp plays for Arsenal.
3. Arsenal will win the cup.

NOT VALID

Aristotle forgot conditional statements that have more than one predicate, e.g.,

"If Socrates is a man, then Socrates is mortal".

We now have two reasons why the argument "Bergkamp plays for Arsenal, therefore Arsenal will win the cup" is false. The first comes from what is actually said. There is no way that the facts that I support Arsenal and that Bergkamp plays for Arsenal are enough to guarantee that Arsenal will win the cup. But there is also the formal reason that the predicate of the first premise is not the subject of the second.

YES, BUT THIS IS VALID ...

1. If I support Arsenal, then they will win the cup.
2. I do support Arsenal, so ...
3. Arsenal will win the cup.

IT IS STILL FALSE BECAUSE VALIDITY ONLY GUARANTEES THE TRUTH OF THE CONCLUSION IF THE PREMISES ARE TRUE. IN YOUR EXAMPLE THE PREMISES ARE FALSE SO THE CONCLUSION REMAINS FALSE.

SO WHAT GOOD DOES THIS FORMALIZATION DO US?

YOU'LL SEE.

Connective Logic

About a hundred years later, **Chrysippus of Soli** (c.280–c.206 BC) changed the focus of logic from single subject-predicate statements to complex statements such as: "Socrates is a man *and* Zeno is a man." This was a major achievement. It was said, "If the gods used logic, it would be the logic of Chrysippus". As we shall see, the same is true of us humans, but it took us a couple of millennia to catch on.

> WITH WORDS LIKE "AND", "OR" AND "IF...THEN...", DIFFERENT STATEMENTS CAN BE JOINED TOGETHER AND THE TRUTH OF THE WHOLE WILL DEPEND EXCLUSIVELY ON THE TRUTH OF THE PARTS.

Each of these *connectives* has a unique way of combining the truth of the parts into the truth of the whole.

For example the "or" connective and only the "or" connective can be used in the following way.

Either Muhammad will go to the mountain

or

the mountain will go to Muhammad.

Muhammad did not go to the mountain, therefore the mountain went to Muhammad.

USING MY DEFINITIONS FOR CONNECTIVES, I CAN SHOW HOW TO DERIVE VARIOUS STATEMENTS WHOSE TRUTH IS ALWAYS GUARANTEED BY THE TRUTH OF THE INITIAL STATEMENT.

Chrysippus had no real impact on the history of logic for at least the next 1,500 years, not least because his writings were lost and his ideas known only by second-hand reports, but also because Aristotle became the darling of the Catholic Church.

Leibniz's Law

For the next 2,000 years, logicians came up with an ever increasing number of syllogisms, some including more than two premises. The logician was a kind of alchemist playing around with concepts to get valid arguments. Eventually, a method in this madness was provided by **Gottfried Leibniz** (1646–1716).

Leibniz came up with the idea of treating statements like equations in algebra. Equations use the equality sign "=" to say that two sides must have the same numerical value,

e.g., $$x^2 + y^2 = z^2$$

Leibniz introduced the equality sign in logic to show that "**a**" is identical with "**b**".

TWO THINGS ARE IDENTICAL IF EVERYTHING THAT CAN BE SAID OF THE ONE CAN BE SAID OF THE OTHER.

IF YOU CAN SAY EXACTLY THE SAME OF TWO THINGS, THEN THEY ARE IDENTICAL.

a = b

This has been known ever since as Leibniz's Law. He analysed it into two inseparable claims, "a is b" and "b is a", which he took to mean that "all **a**'s are **b**'s" and "all **b**'s are **a**'s",

e.g., "All bachelors are unmarried men and all unmarried men are bachelors."

Clearly if **a** is identical with **b**, then we can replace the symbol "a" in any statement with the symbol "b", whilst preserving the truth value of the statement. For example: "Socrates is an unmarried man, an unmarried man is the same as a bachelor, so Socrates is a bachelor."

This is important because it allows us to assess the truth value of a potentially infinite number of sentences using a manageable number of steps. Leibniz had four.

1. "a = a"
e.g., "Socrates is Socrates."

2. If "a is b" and "b is c" then "a is c"

e.g., "All men are mortal, Socrates is a man, therefore Socrates is mortal."

Saying "a is b" is the same as saying that "all a's are b".

SO THIS HAS EXACTLY THE SAME FORM AS MY FIRST SYLLOGISM!

AH, BUT THERE ARE STEPS 3 AND 4 ...

3. "a = not (not a)"
e.g., "If Socrates is mortal then Socrates is not immortal."

4. " 'a is b' = 'not-b is not-a'"
e.g., "Socrates is a man means that if you are not a man then you are not Socrates."

From these simple laws, Leibniz could prove every possible syllogism. Instead of Aristotle's square of oppositions, Leibniz came up with the first real truth theory – deriving conclusions from pre-established laws by substituting identical symbols (synonyms) with each other.

The *Reductio ad Absurdum*

Leibniz's preferred method of proof is an immensely important tool much loved by logicians and philosophers ever since. He called it *reductio ad absurdum*.

The "*reductio*" is a very simple yet fantastically powerful tool. It has been used extensively since Leibniz invented it. It is well illustrated by example.

In the *reductio* method
we assume a statement
to be true and see what
conclusions we can
draw from it. If, when drawing these conclusions, we get a
contradiction, we know that the
initial statement is false, because
contradictions are always false.

SOME PEOPLE DON'T
LIKE MY WONDERFUL NEW
METHOD BECAUSE IT ASSUMES THAT
EVERY SENTENCE IS EITHER TRUE OR
FALSE, AND OFFERS NO SUPPORT
FOR THIS ASSUMPTION.

truefalse

The great advantage of the
reductio method is that it allows
us to tell if a statement is true,
even if we do not know how to
construct a proof for it. We can
tell a statement is true by
showing that its negation leads to
a contradiction.

A "New Organon"

"For my invention used reason in its entirety and is, in addition, a judge of controversy, an interpreter of notions, a balance of probabilities, a compass which will guide us over the ocean of experiences, an inventory of things, a table of thoughts, a microscope for scrutinising things, a telescope for predicting distant things, a general calculus, an innocent magic, a non-chimerical cabal, a script which all will read in their own language and which will lead the way for the true religion everywhere it goes."

Letter from Leibniz to the Duke of Hanover, 1679

THIS IS A REVOLUTION. ARISTOTLE'S OLD ORGANON IS DEAD, INSTEAD I GIVE YOU A *"NEW ORGANON"*. IT IS A NEW WAY OF THINKING ABOUT THE WORLD AND ABOUT LOGIC.

LOGIC IS NO LONGER A TOOL FOR CONVINCING ARGUMENTS BUT RATHER A SYSTEM OF RULES OF THOUGHT, SO THAT EVEN GOD'S THOUGHT IS NECESSARILY LOGICAL. EVEN HE COULD NOT CREATE A WORLD WHERE A CONTRADICTION IS TRUE.

Perhaps unsurprisingly, the Church dubbed him a heretic. But the idea of necessary rules of thought proved to have a lasting influence on Western philosophers like Kant, Hegel, Marx and Russell.

WE ALL TRIED TO GIVE AN ACCOUNT OF WHAT THIS ESSENTIAL LOGIC OF THOUGHT MIGHT BE.

IT SHOULD BE NOTED, HOWEVER, THAT LEIBNIZ'S SYSTEM IS NOT AN *ORGANON* (TOOL) AT ALL. IT IS A CANON OR CODE OF LAWS THAT ORIGINATES IN THINKING BUT THAT NECESSARILY APPLIES TO THE WORLD.

KANT

RUSSELL

HEGEL

MARX

Frege's Quantifiers

The Encyclopaedia of Philosophy says that modern logic began in 1879 with the publication of Gottlob Frege's *Begriffsschrift*. It introduces a propositional calculus which combines Leibniz's proof theory with an account of logical connectives. So we did finally get to Chrysippus.

But the most significant of Frege's new inventions was the *quantifier*. Quantifiers are words like: "**all**", "**some**", "**many**" and "**most**". They allow us to say things about groups of objects, e.g., "**Some men are bald**." Aristotle treated them as subjects to be predicated in a statement, but this can lead to some silly results, like this one from Lewis Carroll's *Alice in Wonderland* ...

"I see nobody on the road," said Alice.

"I only wish I had such eyes," the King remarked in a fretful tone. "To be able to see Nobody! And at that distance too! Why, it's as much as I can do to see real people ..."

Frege manages to avoid this problem by treating quantifiers as logically separate entities.

He used two quantifiers: "**all**" and "**there is at least one**". This allows him to translate

"I see nobody on the road"

as either

"For all people I cannot see them on the road"

or

"There is not at least one person such that I can see them on the road".

Whilst this is no pretty solution, it does allow us to avoid Wonderland-style silliness in logic.

IT SHOWS US WHY "I SEE NOBODY ON THE ROAD" IS ACTUALLY QUITE DIFFERENT FROM "I SEE A MESSENGER ON THE ROAD".

THE WORD "NOBODY" DOES NOT HAVE TO REFER TO AN OBJECT.

The Context Principle

Frege suggested "the context principle" which says that the smallest unit that logic can deal with is a subject-predicate statement, or *proposition*. It is only in the context of a proposition *as a whole* that we know the meanings of the words which compose it.

Take the sentence "I feel cold". This sentence could be uttered by various people at various times. The same words "I feel cold" can be used to express very different propositions, depending upon the circumstances in which they are *used*.

Proposition 1

I FEEL COLD.

Proposition 2

I FEEL COLD.

IT SAYS SOMETHING VERY DIFFERENT WHEN SAID BY SOCRATES AFTER DRINKING POISONOUS HEMLOCK THAN WHEN SAID BY A SMALL CHILD.

Propositional Calculus

Because the fundamental unit of Frege's logic is the proposition, it is known as Propositional Calculus. With it we can assess the truth of complex propositions using connectives. But, more than this, Frege showed that the connectives themselves are truth-related. A proposition using one connective, e.g., "**if...then...**", may be transformed into an expression using the other connectives "**and**" and "**not**" without changing the truth of the complex statement.

"IF YOU ARE A BIRD, THEN YOU HAVE WINGS" ...

... COULD BE REPHRASED ...

... "YOU CANNOT BE A BIRD AND NOT HAVE WINGS".

Frege's logic combines the virtues of Chrysippus (it allows the analysis of sentences in terms of logically connected simple ones) and Leibniz (the ability to prove one statement from another by substituting synonyms), and opens the way to extend these ideas to include the equivalence of different connectives. But Frege's first love was an attempt to deduce mathematics from logic.

Cantor's Set Theory

Gottlob Frege (1848–1925) lived at a time of great mathematical and scientific invention. Among the new and disparate branches of mathematics, patterns were emerging. This led to an attempt to base all of mathematics on one set of rules from which every statement could be derived. Frege thought that his propositional calculus would fit the bill nicely, but it lacked the tools for formulating numbers – without which there is only so far you can go in the formulation of mathematics. Frege's quantifiers "all" and "there is at least one" cannot do the work. An apparent solution came from one of the new branches of mathematics: *Set Theory*, developed by **Georg Cantor** (1845–1918), a contemporary of Frege.

SETS ARE THE MOST BASIC MATHEMATICAL THINGS IMAGINABLE.

They are basically collections of elements that do not need to have anything in common. Every collection has a specific number of elements which can be compared with the number of elements in other sets.

First, we can talk about the common elements of sets **a** and **b**.

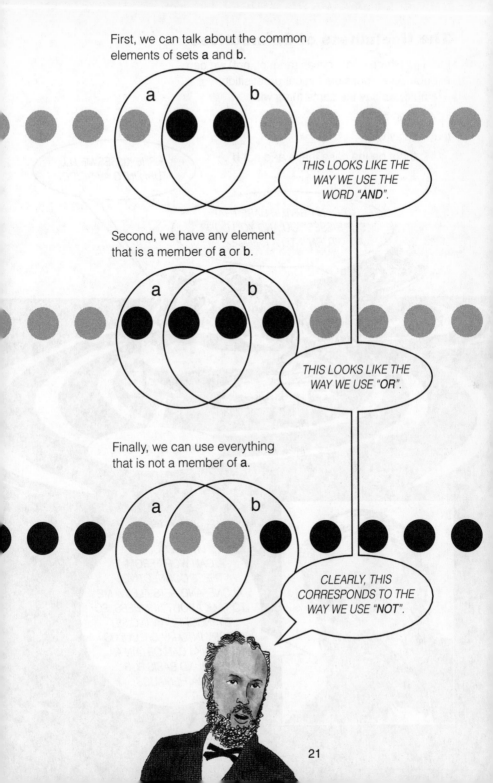

THIS LOOKS LIKE THE WAY WE USE THE WORD "AND".

Second, we have any element that is a member of **a** or **b**.

THIS LOOKS LIKE THE WAY WE USE "OR".

Finally, we can use everything that is not a member of **a**.

CLEARLY, THIS CORRESPONDS TO THE WAY WE USE "NOT".

The Usefulness of Connectives

From just three connectives (**and**, **or**, **not**) we can express every possible logical proposition. For example, we say the same thing with

"if **a** then **b**"

that we say with

"it cannot be the case that **a** and not-**b**".

IF SHE KISSES ME I'LL TURN INTO A PRINCE.

IT CAN'T BE THE CASE THAT SHE KISSES YOU AND YOU DON'T TURN INTO A PRINCE.

THAT'S WHAT I SAID.

MY CALCULUS CAN WORK FROM THESE CONNECTIVES ALONE, AND SETS ALLOW ME TO TALK ABOUT NUMBERS. SO BY INCORPORATING SET THEORY INTO MY CALCULUS I THINK I CAN OBTAIN A SOUND BASIS FOR MATHEMATICS.

The Russell Paradox

As Frege was about to publish his theory, to which he had devoted a good portion of his life, a young English upstart called **Bertrand Russell** (1872–1970) pointed out that Frege's use of sets leads to a fatal contradiction.

The Fatal Flaw

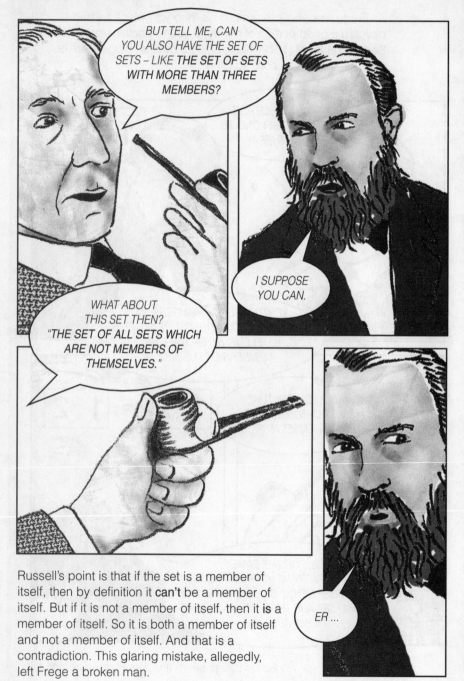

BUT TELL ME, CAN YOU ALSO HAVE THE SET OF SETS – LIKE *THE SET OF SETS WITH MORE THAN THREE MEMBERS?*

I SUPPOSE YOU CAN.

WHAT ABOUT THIS SET THEN? *"THE SET OF ALL SETS WHICH ARE NOT MEMBERS OF THEMSELVES."*

ER ...

Russell's point is that if the set is a member of itself, then by definition it **can't** be a member of itself. But if it is not a member of itself, then it **is** a member of itself. So it is both a member of itself and not a member of itself. And that is a contradiction. This glaring mistake, allegedly, left Frege a broken man.

The Problem of Surface Grammar

Nevertheless, Russell saw merit in Frege's work. With his friend A.N. Whitehead, he tried to ground mathematics on sets and logic. It took a lot of time to avoid contradictions like Frege's. They filled two volumes to attempt a solution! They wanted to ground the fact that 1+1=2 on something more self-evident…

subject verb
object noun a
LOGIC

IT GAVE ME AN IDEA THAT COULD REVOLUTIONIZE PHILOSOPHY! LANGUAGE ITSELF WAS THE PROBLEM! THE SURFACE GRAMMAR OF SENTENCES HIDES THEIR TRUE LOGICAL FORM.

The surface grammar (the school grammar of nouns, verbs and adjectives) hides the true form of a sentence. Russell thought that if we could analyse language into a perfect logical structure, then many of the great philosophical problems of the day would disappear.

Russell's System

Russell brought predicates back into the calculus and developed Frege's conception of quantifiers. This allowed him to distinguish "all" from "some" and it removed the need to analyse existence as a predicate – which could cause a collection of problems. He also formalized Aristotle's square of oppositions by formulating the relations between quantifiers.

If we say that "all birds have wings", and that "there is not one thing that is a bird and does not have wings", then we have said the same thing. The quantifiers "all" and "there is at least one" are interchangeable – one can be substituted for the other with negation symbols in the relevant places.

MINE IS THE FIRST SYSTEM IN WHICH YOU CAN DO ANYTHING YOU COULD DO IN ANY SYSTEM OF LOGIC THAT CAME BEFORE.

Take this sentence:

"The present King of France is bald."

Is this true or false? It could appear as true, false or as neither. But if it is false, does that mean that the present King of France is not bald? Of course, if it is neither true nor false, that means that the sentence does not make any claim at all. It simply does not say anything about the world.

Russell thought that this sentence is actually made up of three combined claims ...

1. There is a present King of France

2. There is exactly one present King of France

3. The present King of France is bald

This combined claim would only be true if all three claims are true. We know that the first condition is false, so the combined claim is also false. But this does not make the opposite claim true, as it may be analysed as follows ...

1. There is a present King of France

2. There is exactly one present King of France

3. The present King of France is **not** bald

And this collection of sentences is clearly false.

Wittgenstein's Logical Pictures

Russell ruled the English philosophy scene for about a decade until an Austrian Jew called **Ludwig Wittgenstein** (1889–1951) gave up a potentially lucrative career in engineering to become a pupil of Russell's in 1912. While on active service during the First World War, he composed the first of his two major works: the *Tractatus Logico-Philosophicus*. This conceived of philosophy as an analysis of hidden logical structure – with definitive attacks on Frege and Russell. Wittgenstein's main interest was always to understand the relation between language, logic and the world.

*THIS CAN BE DONE IF WE SEE LANGUAGE AS A **PICTURE** OF THE WORLD.*

He read in the papers that in Paris law courts, models of cars were used to represent the actual location of vehicles in road traffic accidents. That gave him a brilliant idea.

What any picture must have in common with reality in order to be able to depict it at all is logical form – the *form of reality*. For Wittgenstein, logic was something that both the world and language must have in common. It is only because language has something in common with the world that it can be used to picture the world, so it is only because of logic that our sentences have meaning at all.

THIS IS PRECISELY WHY OUR SENTENCES ARE IN PERFECT LOGICAL ORDER. THIS IS GUARANTEED BY THE FACT THAT OUR SENTENCES HAVE **MEANING**.

Ceci n'est pas une pipe.

IT'S TRUE, THIS IS NOT A PIPE. BUT IT **IS** A LOGICAL REPRESENTATION OF ONE.

A picture that does not have logical form simply does not represent anything at all. Just as a Pollock or Rothko abstract painting does not picture reality.

"It used to be said that God could create anything except an illogical world but the truth is that we could not say of an illogical world what it would look like."

(**Tractatus** 3.031).

29

Carnap and the Vienna Circle

Logic, since Frege, has developed in conjunction with the problem of founding mathematics and solving problems in language. With **Rudolf Carnap** (1891–1970) the emphasis was mainly on science. Originally a pupil of Frege's, but greatly influenced by Wittgenstein's *Tractatus*, Carnap was one of the superstars of the Vienna Circle (a group of philosophers and scientists who wanted to purge philosophy of anything that was neither scientifically verifiable nor a law of logic). "Philosophy is to be replaced by the logic of science and the logic of science is the logical syntax of the language of science." (Carnap, *The Logical Syntax of Language*, 1934)

Carnap deployed his formidable logical skill trying to develop a rigorous account of any possible formal language.

I SAW THIS AS A NECESSARY PRECURSOR TO THE ONLY LEGITIMATE FORM OF PHILOSOPHICAL ENQUIRY – **LOGICAL** ANALYSIS.

METAPHYSICS! METAPHYSICS!

Unfortunately this idea restricted language to such an extent that the Vienna Circle often found it hard to express their views. "...we appointed one of us to shout 'M' (for metaphysics) whenever an illegitimate sentence was uttered in our discussion. He was shouting 'M' so much that we got sick of it and got him to shout 'not-M' whenever we said something legitimate."

The Tolerance Principle

READING THE **TRACTATUS** INSPIRED ME TO THINK THAT I COULD DERIVE ALL MEANINGFUL SENTENCES FROM LOGIC AND SENSE-EXPERIENCE ALONE.

TRACTATUS LOGICO-PHILOSOPHICUS

THIS IS NOT EXACTLY THE MESSAGE OF MY BOOK. MY ACCOUNT OF MEANING CAME FROM THE **WORLD**, NOT FROM SENSE-EXPERIENCE.

Carnap's bid to reduce all language began to flounder almost as soon as he began to work out its consequences. As an older man, having already produced one very long book (the *Aufbau*) to defend his radical approach, Carnap came to relax his view as outlined in another very long book (*Logical Syntax*).

Carnap's most important contribution to the history of logic and formal languages is the introduction of the "tolerance principle", according to which there is not one but *many* logics. Any expression in language is acceptable as long as there are sufficient rules governing its logical application.

Hilbert's Proof Theory

Frege and Russell's attempts to reduce maths to logic and set theory are part of many attempts in the early 20th century to base maths on solid logical grounds. Another notable attempt came from **David Hilbert** (1862–1943), who pioneered a form of logic called "Proof Theory" or *metamathematics*.

Hilbert was interested in what the different branches of mathematics had in common. Every mathematical branch starts with a number of axioms or statements that are just assumed to be true and from which all other statements in that branch can be proven.

> *AS LONG AS NONE OF THE AXIOMS CONTRADICT ONE ANOTHER, THEY MAY BE USED TO CONSTRUCT A POSSIBLE BRANCH OF MATHEMATICS.*

> *I WANT TO FIND A WAY OF PROVING THE CONSISTENCY OF **ANY** LIST OF AXIOMS.*

TRIGONOMETRY

ARITHMETIC

Any branch of mathematics that passed the Hilbert test would be proven to rest on a sound basis.

C O N S I S

The Arrival of Gödel

Broadly speaking, Hilbert's method rests on the idea that we could unquestionably establish the consistency of something like geometry, say, if we could show that we cannot derive from its axioms something equivalent to saying "1=0", which is a prime mathematical absurdity. Hilbert, like Leibniz before him, used the *reductio* as his main tool.

Hilbert's efforts to find a mechanism to prove consistency led to little more than preliminary results. But they did attract the attention of yet another young Austrian, **Kurt Gödel** (1906–78), who was destined to become the greatest logician of the 20th century.

GEOMETRY

CALCULUS

AT THE AGE OF 23, I PROVED THAT ALL THE PROPOSITIONS OF RUSSELL'S PREDICATE CALCULUS ARE TRUE, BUT ALSO THAT EVERY TRUE STATEMENT IS PROVABLE IN THIS LOGIC. TO USE A BIT OF JARGON: IT IS BOTH "COHERENT AND COMPLETE".

T E N C Y

This discovery marked the start of ten intensive years of publication which exerted a profound influence on all subsequent developments in logic and the foundations of mathematics.

Gödel's Incompleteness Theorem

When Gödel was 24 and trying to expand his results to cover arithmetic, he ended up with a thoroughly unexpected result. He discovered that any system complicated enough to be used as a basis for arithmetic will be *incomplete*. This means that Hilbert's project of grounding mathematics on a finite number of axioms could never get off the ground for arithmetic, let alone anything more complicated like calculus.

At this time, Gödel lived a hand-to-mouth existence in Vienna, working in an unpaid position. After the arrival of the Nazis, his friends and colleagues gradually escaped to America. The apolitical Gödel was reluctant to leave – until he was found fit to serve in the army, despite his rampant hypochondria. At which point, he promptly fled.

Gödel's ingenious proofs mark the start of modern mathematical logic. His work has dictated the course of logic up to the present day.

I FINALLY ARRIVED AT PRINCETON UNIVERSITY WHERE I TEAMED UP WITH ALBERT EINSTEIN AND OSKAR MORGENSTERN TO FORM WHAT WAS, IF I DO SAY SO MYSELF, THE MOST BRILLIANT MATHEMATICS DEPARTMENT IN AMERICA.

The Connections to Proof Theory

Modern logic may be divided into three connected projects. These are: *mathematical* logic, *symbolic* logic and *philosophical* logic.

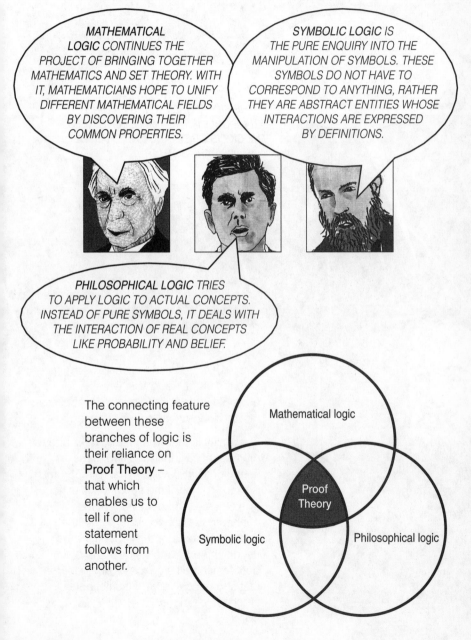

MATHEMATICAL LOGIC CONTINUES THE PROJECT OF BRINGING TOGETHER MATHEMATICS AND SET THEORY. WITH IT, MATHEMATICIANS HOPE TO UNIFY DIFFERENT MATHEMATICAL FIELDS BY DISCOVERING THEIR COMMON PROPERTIES.

SYMBOLIC LOGIC IS THE PURE ENQUIRY INTO THE MANIPULATION OF SYMBOLS. THESE SYMBOLS DO NOT HAVE TO CORRESPOND TO ANYTHING, RATHER THEY ARE ABSTRACT ENTITIES WHOSE INTERACTIONS ARE EXPRESSED BY DEFINITIONS.

PHILOSOPHICAL LOGIC TRIES TO APPLY LOGIC TO ACTUAL CONCEPTS. INSTEAD OF PURE SYMBOLS, IT DEALS WITH THE INTERACTION OF REAL CONCEPTS LIKE PROBABILITY AND BELIEF.

The connecting feature between these branches of logic is their reliance on **Proof Theory** – that which enables us to tell if one statement follows from another.

Mathematical logic

Proof Theory

Symbolic logic

Philosophical logic

Proof Theory contains a variety of methods to show what logically follows from a logical sentence or "formula" – a string of symbols connected by bits of logical syntax. It does this by giving rigid definitions to bits of logical syntax.

THE LOGICAL SYNTAX WILL AFFECT THE TRUTH OF A STATEMENT. SO I DEFINED PIECES OF LOGICAL SYNTAX IN TERMS OF TRUTH AND FALSITY.

FOR EXAMPLE, THE LOGICAL CONNECTIVE "&" IN "THE SKY IS GREY & IT IS RAINING" IS TRUE ONLY IF THE SIMPLE SENTENCES "THE SKY IS GREY" AND "IT IS RAINING" ARE BOTH TRUE.

The idea of defining logical connectives in terms of truth and falsity really took off amongst logicians, so much so that almost nobody has seen fit to change it.

The reality is that when Frege talks about the truth of "&", the *meaning* of the sentence is irrelevant. What is important is that we know if the sentence is either true or false. The behaviour of the connective is unaffected by what the sentence *says*. For this reason, Frege used simple symbols, like p and q, to do duty for whole sentences – another idea that soon became very fashionable amongst logicians.

Wittgenstein's Table of Logical Connectives

Wittgenstein invented a method of representing logical connectives as a simple table, and so saved everyone the bother of using Frege's verbose machinery.

Suppose we represent "**The sky is grey**" as "**p**" and "**It is raining**" as "**q**". Each of them may be either true or false, so altogether we have four possibilities, which may be represented as follows.

p	q
T	T
T	F
F	T
F	F

We can extend this table to show the way that the connective "&" works in the sentence "**p&q**".

WHEN "p" IS TRUE AND "q" IS TRUE THEN "p&q" WILL BE TRUE. BUT WHEN ONE OR BOTH ARE FALSE, THE COMPLEX SENTENCE CANNOT BE TRUE, WHICH GIVES US THE SIMPLE TABLE ...

p	q	p&q
T	T	T
T	F	F
F	T	F
F	F	F

Wittgenstein's Truth Tables

These ideas give us two things: one is mostly relevant to logicians, whilst the other is relevant to all of us in our everyday lives. Logicians use truth tables simply to represent the truth of any logically connected string of sentences. But perhaps more important to our everyday lives is the fact that these connectives lie at the base of much of modern electronics. To begin to grasp either application, we need to understand two more logical connectives.

> THESE TOO MAY BE REPRESENTED BY MY TRUTH TABLE METHOD. TRUTH TABLES CAN BE USED TO DEFINE THE CONNECTIVES THEY REPRESENT.

The first connective we need is "v" (read "or") which may be defined as ...

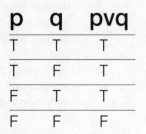

p	q	pvq
T	T	T
T	F	T
F	T	T
F	F	F

This connective is true if either "p" or "q" is true and it is only false when both are false. It roughly corresponds to "and/or" in English.

The other connective we need is "¬" (read "not") which only applies to one sentence. Its Truth Table looks like this ...

p	¬p
T	F
F	T

"¬" roughly corresponds to the English "It is not the case that", as in "It is not the case that Clinton is President of the United States."

Discovering Tautologies

Logical symbols may be used in combination, which can help us calculate the truth condition of any logically complex sentences. For example, "**p ∨ ¬p**", which produces the following Truth Table:

p	¬p	p ∨ ¬p
T	F	T
F	T	T

When a formula only has **T**'s under it in a Truth Table, it means that it is true in all situations. The sentence "**Either it is raining or it is not raining**" cannot be false. Logicians call this a *tautology*.

WITH MY TRUTH TABLES, YOU CAN EASILY DISCOVER ALL THE TAUTOLOGIES THAT CAN BE EXPRESSED USING SIMPLE SYMBOLS.

In a tautology, one truth follows from another of necessity only because of the logical syntax. So we know that any sentence with the same logical syntax will always be true. This is important to Proof Theory because it provides us with a sound base for proving that a logical argument is necessarily true.

The Logic Gates of Digital Electronics

Modern life would be unrecognizable without digital electronics and digital electronics is not a lot more than an instantiation of logic. Digital electronics can be found everywhere from microwaves to mobile phones. Digital electronics relies on "**logic gates**" – basically switches – that let current through, depending on their input. For example, an "And Gate" has *two inputs* and *one output* but will only let current through if there is current at both of the inputs. The behaviour of an And Gate may be represented as follows ...

Input 1	Input 2	Output
1	1	1
1	0	0
0	1	0
0	0	0

AGAIN, MY TRUTH TABLES PROVE USEFUL.

An **And Gate** has exactly the same Truth Table as the logical connective "**&**". Just as the meaning of the sentences was unimportant when looking at the behaviour of "**&**", so the amount of current is unimportant to the behaviours of **And Gates**. Pretty much all digital electronics is constructed out of "**And Gates**", "**Or Gates**" and "**Not Gates**", which correspond to the logical connectives "**&**", "**v**" and "**¬**". They are immensely powerful tools based on logic.

A Vending Machine

Just as logical formulae are constructed out of logical connectives, so logic gates may be used to construct devices like vending machines and ATM's.

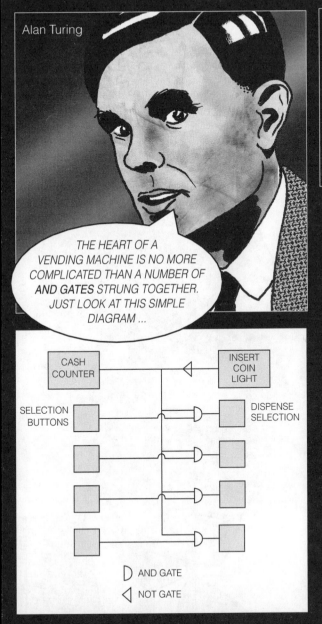

Alan Turing

*THE HEART OF A VENDING MACHINE IS NO MORE COMPLICATED THAN A NUMBER OF **AND GATES** STRUNG TOGETHER. JUST LOOK AT THIS SIMPLE DIAGRAM ...*

The cash counter is a simple device that checks if there is enough money in the machine. When there is enough money it gives out a signal "1", the rest of the time it outputs "0". If the output is "0" then the Not Gate will reverse it and turn on the "insert coin" light. If the cash counter outputs "1" then the Not Gate would turn off the "insert coin" light, and each of the And Gates receives one input at "1". When a product is selected, the corresponding And Gate's second input becomes "1" and it now gives out a "1" signal, releasing the product of choice.

Turing and the "Enigma Code"

The actions of the vending machine follow necessarily from the actions of the buyer. We can also see the actions of the machine as the proof of a given formula. This idea predates logic gates. It comes from **Alan Turing**'s (1912–54) attempts to crack the Enigma Machine, an ingenious German encryption device that was thought foolproof in World War II.

> THE GERMAN TRICK WAS TO ALTER THE CODE VERY REGULARLY. THE FIRST LINE OF THE MESSAGE TOLD THE MACHINE WHAT THE CODE WAS, BUT THIS MESSAGE COULD ONLY BE DECODED BY A MACHINE THAT WAS BUILT THE RIGHT WAY.

Turing tried to crack any possible Enigma code, not just the code for any given message. He was looking for a programmable machine that could have its settings changed, and this would eventually become the computer. But it took about 20 years for his idea to be realized in electronic form.

In essence, computers are nothing more than giant logical "proving" devices.

Euclid's Axiomatic Method

Truth Tables are a good way to model simple electronic devices. But when it comes to doing logic, the prospect of proving a formula using a thirty-line Truth Table is hardly appetizing. Happily, there are other methods.

The first, most common official method of serious modern logic is the "axiomatic" method of proof. It is based on the idea that we can derive all logical tautologies from two or three simple statements that are taken to be true. It owes its origins to Euclid (325–265 BC), the ancient Greek mathematician.

G

H

A

K

B

C

D

L

E

*ALL THE STATEMENTS IN MY FAMOUS BOOK ON GEOMETRY FOLLOW FROM **FIVE SIMPLE STATEMENTS** THAT I TOOK TO BE BOTH FUNDAMENTAL AND TRUE. I CALLED THESE STATEMENTS*

AXIOMS.

Euclid's system is still taught in schools today. His method of constructing a system has taken on a life of its own, since the results it generates are amazingly convincing. This is because the axiomatic method works like a "truth pump" – it makes truth flow from the axioms to the proven statements. The truth of every proven statement is guaranteed by the truth of the axioms.

I CHOSE THE MOST SELF-EVIDENT AXIOMS I COULD, AS THE MORE CERTAIN WE ARE OF THE TRUTH OF THE AXIOMS, THE MORE CERTAIN WE CAN BE OF THE STATEMENTS DERIVED FROM THEM.

I DEVELOPED MY LOGIC FROM EUCLID'S SYSTEM BASED ON FOUR AXIOMS THAT BECAME PART OF THE CANON FOR ALL LATER DEVELOPMENTS.

Aristotle was not overly fond of mathematics, so during his posthumous thousand-year reign over Western philosophy, Euclid's method was put to little use outside mathematics. Galileo first thought of applying it to physics with famously groundbreaking results. He was soon followed by the French philosopher **René Descartes** (1596–1650) who applied it to philosophy, thereby kick-starting the Enlightenment. It was then only a matter of time before Leibniz used it as a proof method in logic.

Leibniz's Proof Method

1. The first axiom is Leibniz's famous law of identity, "**everything is identical with itself**", or "**a = a**".

   The rest are reworkings of some of Aristotle's rules.

2. The "**law of non-contradiction**" which says that no statement is both true and false at the same time, or "**¬(p&¬p)**".

3. The "**law of excluded middle**" which says that every statement is either true or false, or "**pv¬p**".

4. A law of substitution which allows us to substitute one expression for another, keeping the same truth-conditions, or "**(a is b) and (b is c) = a is c**".

> *TAKEN TOGETHER, THE LAWS OF **NON-CONTRADICTION** AND **EXCLUDED MIDDLE** GUARANTEE THAT ANY STATEMENT THAT CAN BE FORMULATED IN LOGIC MUST HAVE ONLY ONE TRUTH VALUE – IT MUST BE EITHER TRUE OR FALSE.*

> *I CAN THEN SAFELY DEDUCE THAT A STATEMENT IS FALSE WHEN IT IS NOT TRUE, A RESULT PRETTY MUCH SELF-EVIDENT.*

> *ARMED WITH THIS AND THE KNOWLEDGE THAT A CONTRADICTION IS **NEVER TRUE**, WE HAVE THE BASIS OF MY **REDUCTIO** METHOD.*

> *WE CAN REJECT ANY STATEMENT THAT LEADS TO A CONTRADICTION AS FALSE.*

Abuse of Contradiction

Logicians worry about contradictions not only because they are always false but also because if they were unavoidable they would destroy the links between the truth of one statement and the truth of another. This is because the Leibnizian *reductio* allows us to prove anything we want from a contradiction.

Suppose we have a contradiction such as **p&¬p** and we want to prove **q** which can stand for any statement we want, such as "elephants only drink bottled water". All we need to do is apply the *reductio* method to ¬q.

So we assume ¬q.

We quote the contradiction **p&¬p**.

p&¬p violates Leibniz's second axiom. The *reductio* method tells us to reject the assumption, which in this case was ¬q.

So we reject the assumption, which gives us ¬¬q.

It follows from the third axiom that if ¬¬q is true, then **q** is true.

This is a weird result because it allows us to prove anything, even something whose truth does not depend on the truth of the contradiction used to prove it.

Rules for Connectives

The application of the axiomatic method reached maturity in Russell and Whitehead's *Principia Mathematica*. The system in this book is a serious contender for grounding mathematics on set theory. The problem is that many of the axioms it uses are far from simple, some are less self-evident than the things they are seeking to prove, e.g., 1+1=2. Nevertheless, a refined version of the method it employed is still in use today, and is called "natural deduction".

WE CAN CONSTRUCT ANY WELL-FORMED LOGICAL FORMULA IF WE KNOW THE CIRCUMSTANCES IN WHICH WE CAN INTRODUCE OR REMOVE A NEW CONNECTIVE FROM THE FORMULA ...

THE BEHAVIOUR OF EACH CONNECTIVE MAY BE EXHAUSTIVELY MAPPED OUT – AS WAS LATER SHOWN BY WITTGENSTEIN'S TRUTH TABLES.

It is a short step from this to a collection of rules that state exactly when we can legitimately introduce a connective. Each connective has one rule for its introduction and one for its elimination. For example, if we have a proposition **q**, and if we can show that taking it to be true leads to a contradiction (the *reductio* method), then we can introduce "¬" to make it "¬**q**". We can eliminate a negation by arriving at a double negative, since ¬¬**p** (it is not the case that it is not the case that the sky is grey) is the same as saying **p** (the sky is grey).

Sensitivity to Grammar

Despite the numerous strengths of natural deduction in Propositional Calculus, it still cannot show why the first of Aristotle's syllogisms is valid. It just cannot cope with the transition from

"All men are mortal"

and

"Socrates is a man"

to

"Socrates is mortal".

The problem is that Propositional Calculus renders whole statements into simple symbols, so "All men are mortal" becomes "p". Because the logical relation between statements like the above seems to depend on the actual wording of the sentences, there is just no way to show the logical dependency between the three symbols that make up Aristotle's first syllogism. For example, if we did a truth table we would not get a tautology.

FOR PRECISELY THIS REASON, I REINTRODUCED ARISTOTLE'S DISTINCTION BETWEEN SUBJECT AND PREDICATE – OBJECTS AND THE THINGS WE SAY ABOUT THEM – INTO MY LOGIC.

NOT THE ACTUAL WORDS, BUT THE STRUCTURE OF THE SENTENCES BECOMES MIRRORED IN THE LOGICAL SYMBOLS.

This might be seen as making logic sensitive to the grammar of the sentences in an argument.

Predicate Calculus

In Russell's Predicate Calculus, lowercase letters stand for objects: a, b, c … stand for specific-named objects and x, y, z stand for as yet unspecified objects. Capitals stand for predicates.

Russell also used special symbols to represent quantifiers: "∀x" stands for "**all**" and "∃x" stands for "**there is at least one**". All the other connectives behave as they did in Propositional Calculus. With this apparatus in place we can account for any possible syllogism.

WHERE ARISTOTLE HAD …

NO HUMAN IS IMMORTAL.
SOCRATES IS HUMAN.
SOCRATES IS MORTAL.

WE HAVE …

$$\forall x \neg (Hx \;\&\; \neg Mx)$$
$$Hs$$
$$Ms$$

We can prove this syllogism using an expanded version of the introduction and elimination rules from Propositional Calculus. Unfortunately we cannot construct Truth Tables to check formulae of Predicate Calculus, as they are simply not equipped to capture the relation between the truth of general statements and the truth of statements that fall under them.

49

Model Theoretic Semantics

Whilst Truth Tables do not work for Predicate Calculus, there are other methods. The most important of them employs very simple models of the world. The model provides us with a way of checking the truth of statements in Predicate Calculus relative to a given list of objects and predicates.

> MODELS ALLOW US TO ATTACH MEANING TO LOGICAL FORMULAE AND SO INVESTIGATE THE TRUTH OF PARTICULAR STATEMENTS RELATIVE TO A GIVEN SITUATION. THIS IS CALLED **MODEL THEORETIC SEMANTICS**. WITHOUT IT, ALL WE CAN DO IS SHOW THAT AN ARGUMENT IS VALID, THAT IF **Px** THEN **Qx**.

> WITH MODEL THEORETIC SEMANTICS WE CAN FIND OUT IN WHAT MODELS "*SOCRATES IS A MAN*" IS TRUE.

> THIS IS A GREAT IDEA, BECAUSE ONCE THE MODEL BECOMES LARGE AND COMPLICATED ENOUGH, WE CAN APPLY IT TO THOUGHT ITSELF. THAT WOULD BE A GREAT HELP IN UNDERSTANDING THE HUMAN MIND AND IN CONSTRUCTING MACHINES THAT CAN EMULATE IT.

But before we can put this semantics to great use, we need a grammatical system on which to pin it. This grammatical system must allow us to construct a potentially infinite number of sentences from a finite number of rules.

A MAN

Hilbert's Recursion Model

Precisely such a tool was developed by Hilbert in his work on the foundations of mathematics. Unimpressed by the idea of reducing mathematics to logic, Hilbert wanted a mathematical version of Proof Theory – a way to prove mathematical statements from within mathematics. The name "Proof Theory" is actually Hilbert's.

IN ARITHMETIC, ANY WELL-FORMED FORMULA CAN BE THE BASIS OF ANY OTHER WELL-FORMED FORMULA, PROVIDING THAT WE FOLLOW THE RULES. FROM 1 + 1 WE CAN ARRIVE AT 1 + 1 + 1.

IN THIS RESPECT, ARITHMETIC IS LIKE ENGLISH, IN WHICH WE CAN CONTINUE TO APPLY WORDS LIKE "**AND**" ...

I'M JUST GOING OUT TO THE SHOPS, CAN I GET YOU ANYTHING?

OH, CAN YOU GET ME SOME GRAPES ...

... AND SOME SCOURING PADS ...

... AND SOME CORN FLAKES ...

... AND SOME BLEACH.

This continued re-application is called **recursion** and is vital for the construction of models. It allows us to construct an infinite number of sentences from a few simple rules and a finite vocabulary.

Hilbert had a view of mathematics that he called *formalism*. The idea is that the things mathematics talks about are nothing but symbols. These symbols are, by themselves, meaningless – you know everything about them when you know how to manipulate them. He gave recursive rules to explain their possible interactions.

THE MOST FAMOUS MATHEMATICAL ENTITY IS THE NUMBER. ALL POSITIVE WHOLE NUMBERS CAN BE CONSTRUCTED FROM TWO SIMPLE RULES:

"1 IS A NUMBER"

AND "ANY NUMBER PLUS 1 IS A NUMBER".

Since mathematicians already know how to construct every number with the help of positive whole numbers and zero, these two rules are, more or less, all you need to construct any number. Hilbert's rules are both simple and effective. In effect, they treat mathematics as a formal language made up of a vocabulary and a syntax. The syntax allows you to create sentences of the language without having a clue to what they mean. The vocabulary is no more than a collection of blanks with grammatical properties: *names, verbs* and the like. Just as we know to put a name with a verb to form a complete sentence in English, even if we do not know whose name it is.

Consider a model language made up only of the following terms ...

Predicates	Names
Evolved into	*Homo sapiens*
	Homo sapiens sapiens
	Homo erectus
	Homo habilis

And the following simple grammatical rules:

1. sentence =
    name, predicate, name

2. sentence =
    sentence, "which", *predicate, name*

The first rule shows how to build a well-formed formula out of the sequence *name, predicate, name*.

For example, "*Homo erectus* evolved into *Homo sapiens*".

The second rule shows how to build a new well-formed formula out of a sentence that already exists and in addition the sequence "which", *predicate, name*.

For example, "*Homo erectus* evolved into *Homo sapiens* which evolved into *Homo habilis*".

Using this model we can construct an infinite number of sentences via the recursive application of Rule Two. Of course only a few of these sentences will be true, but it should now be clear that this familiar diagram is yet another application of logic.

Finite Rules for Infinite Production

The American philosopher **Donald Davidson** (b.1917) has suggested that we can apply this idea to English and every other natural language, filling in the gaps with a semantic model.

"We must give an account of how the meanings of sentences depend on the meanings of words. Unless such an account could be supplied for a particular language, there would be no explaining the fact that we can learn that language: no explaining the fact that on mastering a finite vocabulary and a finitely stated set of rules, we are prepared to produce and understand a potential infinitude of sentences." (*Truth and Meaning*, 1966)

Languages like English are potentially infinite, if we continue to apply words like "and".

> EITHER THERE IS A FINITE OR AN INFINITE NUMBER OF RULES GOVERNING EACH POSSIBLE USE OF THE WORD "**AND**". IF THE RULES WERE INFINITE, THEN WE COULD NOT LEARN THEM.

We must be able to apply the rules recursively in order to produce a potentially infinite number of sentences. Davidson concludes that English, or any other language that we actually use, could be described as a huge model. So the application of formal languages to natural languages gets a philosophical seal of approval.

All you need to know about the word AND

> BUT IF THERE IS ONLY A FINITE NUMBER OF RULES, THEN THEY CAN BE LEARNED.

RULES FOR THE WORD 'AND'

RULES FOR THE WORD 'AND'

RULES FOR THE WORD 'AND'

RULES FOR THE WORD 'AND'

RULES FOR THE WORD 'AND'

RULES FOR THE WORD 'AND'

RULES FOR THE WORD 'AND'

RULES FOR THE WORD 'AND'

RULES FOR THE WORD 'AND'

RULES FOR THE WORD 'AND'

WORD 'AND'

RD 'AND'

RULE AND'

Simple Instructions

If Davidson is right, then language is a bit like Lego. It is made up of blocks (words) that have to be combined correctly. Instructions for how to connect one block to another will give the instructions to build any possible Lego structure.

What Davidson is really interested in is how the meaning of each individual word contributes to the meaning of the sentence. For example, the sentence ...

can be analysed as

"There is an event in which I walked and the event happened slowly"

$(\exists x)(Wx\&Sx)$.

Here is an analysis of a statement in English – built out of the conjunction of two simple statements which consist of a subject and a predicate.

Davidson's account has two principal virtues. First, it neatly fits his learnability conditions. Second, it provides an account of language that preserves much of our intuitive grasp on natural language. For example, "I am walking" follows from "I am walking slowly" because in Proof Theory "**Wx**" follows from "Wx&Sx".

Davidson devoted more than a decade to analysing different parts of language into this sort of logical form.

Proof Theory and Formal Language

Davidson encourages us to think of all adjectives, adverbs and prepositions as predicates strung together. This contrasts with Russell's analysis of those linguistic terms.

I SAY THAT "I WENT SKIING WITH A FRIEND" IS A SINGLE PREDICATE THAT SAYS SOMETHING ABOUT TWO SUBJECTS. A PREDICATE LIKE "WENT SKIING WITH" ONLY MAKES SENSE IF THERE ARE TWO SUBJECTS ATTACHED.

BUT RUSSELL, HOW CAN YOU ACCOUNT FOR THE FACT THAT "I WENT SKIING WITH A FRIEND" ACTUALLY ENTAILS "I WENT SKIING"?

I CAN'T, BECAUSE IN PROOF THEORY THERE IS NO WAY TO ACCOUNT FOR THE ENTAILMENT FROM A TWO PLACE PREDICATE TO A ONE PLACE PREDICATE. PROOF THEORY LACKS THE RELEVANT SEMANTIC MACHINERY.

At root, Davidson is trying to understand English as a formal language. To do this, he needs a way of deciding under what conditions sentences of English are true.

Davidson adopted an account of truth in formal languages developed by a Berkeley colleague, **Alfred Tarski** (1902–83). Tarski developed a distinction between the *formal* language and the language used to *speak about* the formal language (the metalanguage).

Tarski's Truth Conditions

Tarski provided a set of conditions that allow us to say when a sentence of a formal language under study is true. The result is startlingly simple.

S IS TRUE IF, AND ONLY IF, p.

In Tarski's schema, "**S**" is a sentence of a formal language and "**p**" is the translation of **S** into the metalanguage. If the metalanguage is English and the formal language contains English sentences, we can say "'**Snow is white**' if, and only if, snow is white."

Tarski's schema looks less trivial if we use it to state the truth conditions of a foreign language: "**La neige est blanche**" is true if and only if snow is white. It looks like we could use the schema to give us the meaning of the French sentence.

THE PREDICATE "IS TRUE" IS NEVER PROPERLY APPLIED WITHIN A FORMAL LANGUAGE, RATHER IT SAYS SOMETHING ABOUT THE SENTENCES OF THE FORMAL LANGUAGE.

La neige est blanche

snow is ← p   S

METALANGUAGE

Snow is white
if, and only if,
Snow is white

Davidson thinks that our understanding of English can be explained by understanding a list of sentences built around Tarski's schema.

> HAVING SUCH A LIST IS ALL THAT IS REQUIRED TO ACCOUNT FOR OUR UNDERSTANDING OF OUR NATURAL LANGUAGE, BECAUSE IF WE KNOW THE CONDITIONS UNDER WHICH A SENTENCE IS TRUE, THEN WE UNDERSTAND HOW TO USE THAT SENTENCE.

So even something as superficially simple as

"'Snow is white' is true if, and only if, snow is white."

is all that is required to begin to do duty for a theory of meaning, according to Davidson. When this is combined with Davidson's attempt to show how the truth conditions of sentences depend on the truth conditions *of their parts,* then the ground is set for working out the truth conditions of every possible sentence in English.

Formal Semantics in Practice

The great practical advantage of formal semantics lies in our ability to build machines that respond to a formally defined language – all computers are such machines.

> ANY COMPUTER LANGUAGE IS COMPOSED OF A VOCABULARY AND RULES DESCRIBING HOW TO MAKE WELL-FORMED STATEMENTS IN THAT LANGUAGE. ALL PROGRAMS WRITTEN IN THE LANGUAGE CONSIST OF SUCH WELL-FORMED STATEMENTS.

But this does not only apply to computers. Modern particle physics is done within formal languages, with quantum theory providing the model. Often we don't even know what the terms used in the model – like photons and electrons – mean outside of the model. Electrons have never been directly observed: their properties define what they are and compose their *formal identity* in scientists' models. The interactions between particles in the model can be seen as *syntactical rules* governing their behaviour. The achievement of physicists is to show that their models correspond to experimental results.

Constructing a Soap Opera

We can construct formal languages to model almost anything. Here is one used to construct the plot of a typical soap opera:

Predicates	Characters	Connectives
Dies	Billy-Anne	and
Has an affair	Esmarelda	or
Is bankrupt	Zulika	because
	Juan	
Loves	John-Bob	
Hates	Eric	
Has an affair with	Dwayne	

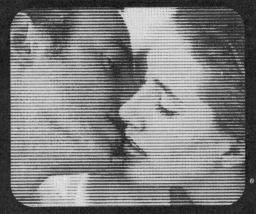

Notice the difference between predicates that take *one* character like "**has an affair**" and those that take *two* like "**has an affair with**". They require separate rules of combination. The connectives do not have to be "logical" in the same way as the connectives of Predicate Calculus, but their behaviour in the language will be exhaustively defined. All possible well-formed formulae may be generated from the following rules ...

1. For one-place predicates:
    sentence = name, predicate

2. For two-place predicates:
    sentence = name, predicate, name

3. For the connectives:
    sentence = simple sentence, connective, simple sentence

From this we can arrive at a potentially infinite number of sentences: "**Juan is bankrupt**", "**Billy-Anne loves Eric**", "**John-Bob dies because Esmarelda has an affair with Zulika**" ...

Prolog to an AI Soap Opera

While all computer languages are formal languages, some show their true nature more blatantly than others. Within most computer languages the vocabulary and grammar are pre-set; but languages like *Prolog* allow the computer to develop its own programming.

THE MOTIVATION COMES FROM MY IDEA THAT MACHINES COULD HAVE SKILLS OF LEARNING, SELF-CORRECTION AND COMMUNICATION.

THIS FORMS THE BASIS OF MOST ATTEMPTS AT CREATING ARTIFICIAL INTELLIGENCE (AI).

With Prolog the idea is simple. The computer is given a model similar to, but more complex than, the soap opera language. The vocabulary is made up of words for the computer to use and instructions for it to perform. The computer can then be set specific tasks based on that vocabulary. It can also identify bits of vocabulary that it does not possess, and ask for them.

Prolog's vocabulary consists of "facts" which are statements composed of predicates and the names of variables – such as:

"Went to the moon (Neil Armstrong)"

and

"Went to the moon (Buzz Aldrin)".

A set of rules is added to give structure and link one fact to another, so ...

"The first man on the moon was Neil Armstrong"

becomes

"The first man on the moon (x):- x = Neil Armstrong".

The final element takes the form of questions in which the machine is set certain tasks, thus

"? first man on the moon"

would receive the answer ...

LANGUAGES LIKE PROLOG CONTAIN EVERYTHING THAT I THOUGHT WAS NEEDED TO CREATE A MACHINE AS INTELLIGENT AS WE ARE.

NEIL ARMSTRONG

Turing's recipe for AI

To prepare an intelligent machine, we need ...

1. A model with a vocabulary rich enough to represent the real
   world.

2. This model will then be used to build a picture of the world.
   You might find a dash of self-learning helpful here.

3. Now we need to put together the input and output devices.
   The input should be composed of devices similar to our own
   senses. The output is comprised of behavioural responses
   appropriate to the world picture we created earlier.

PRESENTED IN THE RIGHT WAY, THIS WOULD BE INDISTINGUISHABLE FROM YOUR NEXT-DOOR NEIGHBOUR.

As well as showing that machines can be programmable, using something like a formal language, Turing also paved the way for building the first digital computers. It was Turing who discovered that vacuum tubes could be used to store information electronically. Up to this point, all his machines had been mechanical. The introduction of the vacuum tube saw cogs replaced by electronics. Today, transistors have replaced vacuum tubes, but the principle remains unchanged.

Turing committed suicide in 1954, perhaps driven to it by brutal treatment from the British legal system. Despite his tremendous contribution to the war effort and his inspired later work on computers and AI, in 1952 Turing was put on trial for "gross indecency" – in short for being gay.

I AVOIDED A PRISON SENTENCE BY PLEADING GUILTY, BUT AS A CONDITION OF MY PAROLE I WAS FORCED TO SUBMIT MYSELF TO OESTROGEN INJECTIONS – A FORM OF CHEMICAL CASTRATION.

The Problem of Paradoxes

As with most things in logic, Proof Theory at first glance looks dry and obscure. Often the practical side of its applications as a method of logical proof seems limited. But it forms the skeleton of much of our science, mathematics and computer technology. One of Proof Theory's virtues is its ability to guarantee a single repeatable result every time it is applied to a particular string of symbols, which is more than can be said for the majority of scientific experiments. However, if the string of symbols in question contains a contradiction, the method's effectiveness breaks down, as *anything* follows from a contradiction.

WHEN RUSSELL DISCOVERED A PARADOX IN MY SYSTEM OF LOGIC, IT MADE EVERYONE, EVEN ME, REJECT THE SYSTEM. THE PARADOX HE DISCOVERED WAS AN UNAVOIDABLE CONTRADICTION BUILT INTO THE SYSTEM.

FREGE BECAME AN OBJECT LESSON FOR LOGICIANS WHO HAVE BEEN TRYING TO AVOID PARADOXES EVER SINCE.

A paradox is a statement that entails its negation. This is a logician's nightmare because it does not matter whether we assume the sentence to be true or false, we always arrive at a contradiction. This makes it very hard to hold onto the law of non-contradiction (no sentence can be both true and false at the same time). The word "paradox" is Greek in origin, and with good reason. Sceptics in ancient Greece wanted to show that reason could not lead to absolute knowledge – the paradox was their principal weapon. The most notorious of these philosophical reprobates was **Zeno of Elea** (c.495–c.430 BC).

PERHAPS THE MOST FAMOUS GREEK PARADOX IS THE SO-CALLED "LIAR PARADOX" WHICH IN ITS MOST SIMPLE FORM LOOKS LIKE THIS ...

This Sentence is False.

The problem here is that if the sentence is true, then it is false; but if it is false, then it must be true. If we assume it to be either true or false, it still leads to a contradiction. This is the most notorious of a family of *self-referential* paradoxes. They are called "self-referential" because the sentence speaks of itself.

Can Paradoxes be Avoided?

Paradoxes pose serious problems for the logical systems of Leibniz, Frege and Russell. They allow the formulation of contradictions within very simple systems. Logicians have tried to avoid the liar paradox in a number of different ways, none of which is very convincing.

ONE ATTEMPT TO AVOID THE LIAR PARADOX IS TO BAR ANY SELF-REFERENTIAL SENTENCES FROM LOGICAL SYSTEMS. BUT THIS HAS TWO PROBLEMS:

1.
SOME SELF-REFERENTIAL SENTENCES ARE TOTALLY HARMLESS, E.G., "*THIS SENTENCE HAS FIVE WORDS*."

2.
WE CAN CONSTRUCT A PARADOX THAT WORKS AS A LIAR PARADOX THAT IS NOT SELF-REFERENTIAL ...

HER SIGN IS FALSE

HIS SIGN IS TRUE

THIS WORKS IN THE SAME WAY AS THE TRADITIONAL LIAR PARADOX. IF HIS SIGN IS TRUE, THEN HER SIGN IS FALSE – AND VICE VERSA.

Theory of Types

Russell's paradox used against Frege is roughly a reformulation of the Liar in the language of Set Theory. Russell asked us to consider the set of all sets that are not members of themselves. The question he raised was whether this set is a member of itself. This leads to the familiar pattern: if it is a member of itself, then it is not a member of itself; if it is not a member of itself, then it is a member of itself. Russell came up with a complicated logical machinery to tackle this problem.

MOST OF MY WORK IN LOGIC WAS DEVOTED TO DEVELOPING THIS MACHINERY. I CALLED IT THE "THEORY OF TYPES".

*WE SHOULD CONTRAST DIFFERENT **TYPES** OF SETS ...*

SETS WHOSE MEMBERS ARE OBJECTS, SETS WHOSE MEMBERS ARE SETS, AND SO ON. WE CAN GO ON INDEFINITELY TO HAVE SETS WHOSE MEMBERS ARE SETS OF SETS AND SUCH LIKE.

MEMBERS OF SETS

OBJECTS

SETS OF SETS

In the same way we can use predicates that talk about objects and predicates that talk about predicates, like: "to be beautiful is dangerous".

Russell's theory argues that if we prohibit crossover between types, then his paradox is solved – the problematic set is a set of sets and as such of a different *type* than the sets that make it up. The paradox does not get off the ground because it involves crossover between types.

Unfortunately, when this solution is applied to the Liar Paradox it turns out that this potentially infinite solution is not enough. When Russell tried to analyse "**This sentence is false**", he found it consisted of two sentences ...

The first says of an object that it is a sentence ...

... and the second says of the sentence that it is false.

Russell thought that "**This is true**" is a predicate that says something about a sentence – i.e., about a predicate and its object.

THE PROBLEM FOR THE SIMPLE THEORY OF TYPES IS THAT THE LIAR HAS **TWO** PREDICATES OF DIFFERENT TYPES – A SITUATION IT CANNOT COPE WITH.

Willard Van Orman Quine (1908–2000)

I DID FIND A WAY TO COPE WITH THIS PROBLEM, BUT ONLY AT THE COST OF MAKING MY SYSTEM EVEN MORE UNWIELDY.

RUSSELL'S NEW SYSTEM PREVENTED SO MANY CROSSOVERS BETWEEN TYPES THAT IT BECAME IMPOSSIBLE TO PROVE EVEN THE ELEMENTARY PROPOSITIONS OF SET THEORY USING THAT SYSTEM.

70

Tarski's Solution to the Liar

Tarski thought that his own distinction between the language "under study" and the "metalanguage" could neatly take care of the Liar, because "is true" and "is false" are predicates of the metalanguage.

When the liar says "this sentence is false", he is misapplying the predicate "is false". He treats it as being part of the object language. But it can only really be applied to the *metalanguage*.

> A SENTENCE CANNOT CONTAIN ITS *OWN TRUTH PREDICATE*. *"THIS SENTENCE IS FALSE"* IS NO MORE A PART OF THE OBJECT LANGUAGE THAN *"SNOW IS BLANCHE"* IS PART OF ENGLISH.

This solution is similar to Russell's, as it does not allow sentences of the same type to speak of their own truth value. Just as there are infinite types, so with Tarski's proposal there are languages to study languages to study the metalanguage and so on indefinitely.

The Unexorcised Paradox

Just as the Liar appeared to be a problem for Russell, so a paradox like "The next sentence is false. The last sentence is true." is problematic for Tarski. One sentence seems to belong to both the metalanguage and to the the metalanguage for the metalanguage.

THE LAST SENTENCE IS TRUE

THE NEXT SENTENCE IS FALSE

"THE NEXT SENTENCE IS FALSE" IS TALKING ABOUT A SENTENCE, SO AT THE VERY LEAST IT BELONGS TO A METALANGUAGE.

"THE LAST SENTENCE IS TRUE" SHOULD BE THE SUBJECT OF DISCUSSION, BUT IT SAYS SOMETHING ABOUT THE SENTENCE OF THE METALANGUAGE. IN SHORT, IT SEEMS TO BELONG TO TWO LANGUAGES AT ONCE.

THE LAST SENTENCE IS TRUE

The Liar remains one of the great unsolved paradoxes. It continues to torment philosophers and logicians alike, inspiring new solutions now and again. It has a peculiar habit of turning up in different contexts at different times.

DO YOU KNOW WHAT *"HETEROLOGIES"* ARE?

THEY ARE WORDS THAT ARE NOT WHAT THEY SAY. FOR EXAMPLE, *"LONG"* IS NOT LONG, *"BIG"* IS NOT BIG, AND SO ON.

THEN IS THE WORD *"HETEROLOGICAL"* HETEROLOGICAL OR NOT?

IF IT'S NOT HETEROLOGICAL, THEN IT IS WHAT IT SAYS IT IS; BUT THEN IT SAYS IT'S HETEROLOGICAL.

AND IF IT IS?

THEN IT IS NOT WHAT IT SAYS; BUT THEN AGAIN IT SAYS IT'S HETEROLOGICAL.

SO IT IS AND IT ISN'T HETEROLOGICAL – A PARADOX, YOU MIGHT SAY.

Heterological

Gödel's Incompleteness Theorem

The most influential of the modern self-referential paradoxes is Gödel's Second Incompleteness Theorem. When it was first published in 1931, few people could understand it. This does not mean that the ideas behind it are particularly hard. Its results have had a huge impact on science, mathematics and philosophy.

Gödel came up with the ingenious idea of encoding the statements of logic and metamathematics as numbers. He assigned every symbol in Russell's logic a number, then inserted the numbers into a mathematical formula that generated a unique number for every possible string of symbols in this logic.

WHEN I WAS STUDYING UNDER HILBERT, I HELPED HIM ON HIS PROJECT TO FIND CONSISTENCY PROOFS FOR ARITHMETIC, USING HIS RECURSIVE METHOD. TO MY SURPRISE, EARLY IN THE SEARCH, I DISCOVERED THAT NO SUCH PROOFS COULD BE PROVIDED.

In Gödel's system we can translate as follows ...

P	v	¬	P
112	2	1	112

This allows Gödel to produce a unique number for this formula.

USING THIS METHOD, I SHOWED THAT A PARTICULAR NUMBER WOULD CORRESPOND TO A FORMULA IN RUSSELL'S FULL SYSTEM THAT SAYS: *"THIS FORMULA IS UNPROVABLE."*

Once we have arrived at this formula, we can go one of two ways. First, suppose this sentence is true – we have a true statement in Russell's logic that cannot be proven. This means that Russell's logic is *incomplete.* Alternatively, if the sentence is false, it means that it is provable – but then a false statement is provable in Russell's logic, so it is *incoherent.*

The Consequences of Gödel's Theorem

Neither of these suggestions is very appealing to Russell or Hilbert, who wanted to construct a system that will produce *all* and *only* true sentences of mathematics. They now faced the fact that this goal is unachievable in principle.

I HAVE SHOWN THAT THE BASIC BRANCHES OF MATHEMATICS MAY BE FORMALIZED BY A SET OF AXIOMS IN ACCORDANCE WITH HILBERT'S PROGRAMME. BUT THE CONCLUSIONS OF MY THEOREM APPLY TO THEM AS WELL. SO EITHER BASIC ARITHMETIC IS INCOMPLETE OR IT IS INCOHERENT – EITHER ONE TRUE CALCULATION CANNOT BE PROVEN OR ONE FALSE ONE CAN.

Gödel's theorem can be generalized to cover any sufficiently complex formal language in which there is a certain "order" among the different sentences. Gödel subsequently went on to prove that mathematics is essentially incomplete – that no list of axioms can ever account for all the truths of arithmetic. The conclusion that there are true sentences of mathematics that cannot be proven is very alarming for anyone interested in trying to set mathematics on a secure basis.

Gödel put the final nail in the 19th-century dream of deriving all mathematics from a simple and rigorous set of axioms. Logic is no longer practised in the hope of grounding mathematics.

> IT IS NOT ALL BAD NEWS FOR THE EVERYDAY PRACTICE OF MATHEMATICIANS. AS LONG AS THEY SHOW THAT THEIR SYSTEMS ARE CONSISTENT, AT THE PRICE OF BEING INCOMPLETE, THEY CAN CONTINUE TO PRODUCE BY FAR THE GREAT MAJORITY OF MATHEMATICAL SENTENCES.

> WHILST MY PROGRAMME WAS DEVASTATED, MY **METHOD** CONTINUED TO BE OF USE IN FORMALIZING AND AXIOMATIZING NEW BRANCHES OF MATHEMATICS. I MYSELF DEVISED A MATHEMATICAL SYSTEM TO DEAL WITH THE BIZARRE REALM OF QUANTUM PARTICLES, WHICH THEY NOW CALL **HILBERT SPACES**.

The "Halting Problem"

Gödel's theorem shows us something very similar when applied to computation. Using Gödel's numbering system, every formal mathematical proof can be transformed into a relatively simple numerical calculation. So to every formula there corresponds a particular number. This means that if there is a formula that cannot be proven, then there is a number that cannot be calculated.

> USING A NEAT MATHEMATICAL TRICK, I SHOWED THAT MY IDEAL COMPUTER COULD NOT COMPUTE MOST NUMBERS, BECAUSE THERE ARE MORE IRRATIONAL NUMBERS SUCH AS π THAN THERE ARE RATIONAL NUMBERS SUCH AS **7**.

> COMPUTERS ARE MACHINES THAT SIMULATE NUMERICAL CALCULATIONS. IT IS BASICALLY MY NUMBERING TECHNIQUE THAT ALLOWS THEM TO RUN PROGRAMS WITHIN FORMAL LOGIC.

This means that Gödel's incompleteness theorem applies to computers. The uncomputable numbers correspond in a way to programs that will never give a result. Gödel's incompleteness theorem means that there cannot be a program using a finite number of steps to check any program to see whether it will reach a conclusion or halt. This has become known as the "halting problem". Such a program would be equivalent to a system in which you could consistently compute all numbers, and that is an impossibility.

The Limit of Gödel's Proof

Despite its wide-ranging ramifications, there are certain things that Gödel's proof cannot do. It does not absolutely guarantee that we could not use Hilbert's method to prove the consistency and completeness of arithmetic, only that such a proof is not capable of being *represented* within arithmetic. This is true, but nobody to date knows what such a proof would look like, let alone how to construct one.

It cannot be used to say, as some have tried, that mysterious intuition must replace cogent proof. Nor is it a proof that there are inherent limits to human reasoning, since no one knows if human reasoning falls under Hilbert's rules.

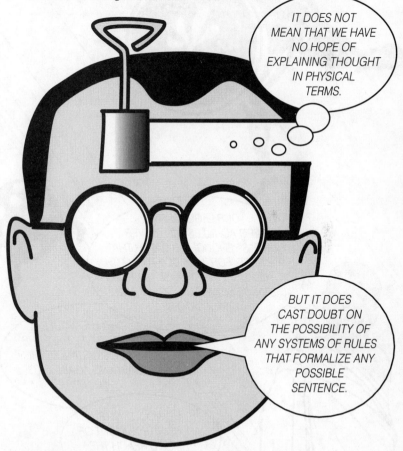

IT DOES NOT MEAN THAT WE HAVE NO HOPE OF EXPLAINING THOUGHT IN PHYSICAL TERMS.

BUT IT DOES CAST DOUBT ON THE POSSIBILITY OF ANY SYSTEMS OF RULES THAT FORMALIZE ANY POSSIBLE SENTENCE.

Gödel's incompleteness theorem has even made it into first-year undergraduate *ethics lectures*.

Zeno's Movement Paradox

The most famous of the non-self-referential paradoxes was also invented by Zeno of Elea. Zeno wanted to show that movement was impossible. Every time we see something move, it is our senses deceiving us. Zeno's principal argument for this curious claim was to show that if movement were to exist, it would lead to a contradiction.

OUR LEGENDARY HERO ACHILLES WILL NEVER RUN FAST ENOUGH TO CATCH THAT TORTOISE. FOR IN ORDER TO CATCH IT, HE MUST FIRST TRAVEL **HALF** THE DISTANCE BETWEEN HIMSELF AND THE TORTOISE.

THEN HE WOULD HAVE TO TRAVEL HALF THE REMAINING DISTANCE; THEN AGAIN AND AGAIN ... TO INFINITY.

HE WOULD TAKE AN INFINITE AMOUNT OF TIME TO REACH THE TORTOISE.

Zeno would claim to have reached his conclusion from true premises. Who would deny that to get from A to B you have to travel half the distance first? But our senses tell us that we reach and pass places all the time. So Zeno concludes that our senses deceive us. Zeno's paradox can be applied to all types of movement.

SINCE AN ARROW SHOT TOWARDS A TARGET FIRST HAS TO COVER HALF THE DISTANCE, AND THEN HALF THE REMAINDER, AND THEN HALF THE REMAINDER AFTER THAT, AND SO AD INFINITUM ...

THE RESULT IS THAT ALTHOUGH AN ARROW IS ALWAYS APPROACHING ITS TARGET, IT NEVER QUITE GETS THERE.

So Saint Sebastian must have died of fright!

An Infinite Sum

Zeno's Paradox relies on an assumption made by all mathematicians before Newton and Leibniz. They assumed that any sum of an infinite number of positive numbers would be infinite. It is an easy assumption to make.

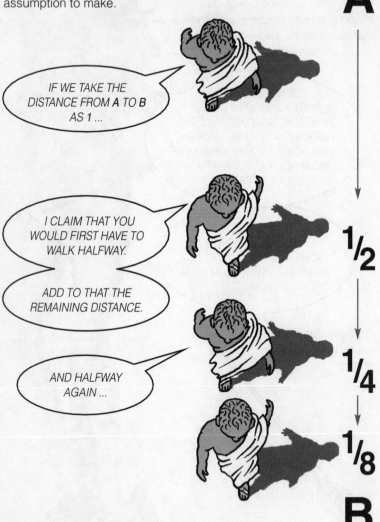

IF WE TAKE THE DISTANCE FROM A TO B AS 1 ...

I CLAIM THAT YOU WOULD FIRST HAVE TO WALK HALFWAY.

ADD TO THAT THE REMAINING DISTANCE.

AND HALFWAY AGAIN ...

The consequence is that we have an infinite sum of positive quantities $1/2 + 1/4 + 1/8 \ldots$ and that, according to Zeno's assumption, would be infinite. We would never get from A to B!

A Convergence on Limits

What Newton and Leibniz discovered almost simultaneously was that often the sum of a positive number of integers is *not* infinite. Some infinite calculations have the property of converging on limits. Which is to say, with each subsequent addition we get ever closer to a *particular* number. Given an infinite number of calculations, we could eventually arrive at the number.

A ⟶ B ⟵ A

UNFORTUNATELY FOR ZENO, THE SUM $1/2 + 1/4 + 1/8 ...$ IS JUST SUCH A CALCULATION.

1

IT CAN EASILY BE SHOWN, USING OUR METHOD, THAT THE FINAL SUM OF THIS CALCULATION IS 1.

This is fortuitous, as it means that it takes exactly the time to get from A to B that it takes to get from A to B ... and our senses are saved.

IT TOOK 2,000 YEARS, BUT EVENTUALLY I BEAT THAT TORTOISE!

How Much is a "Heap"?

The other famous non-self-referential paradox is the **Sorites** or **Heap paradox**. It was much loved by the Stoics who used it to show the weakness of reason. It relies on the fact that some words in our language, like "heap", are vague. In certain instances, there are no sharp rules to say when they can be applied correctly.

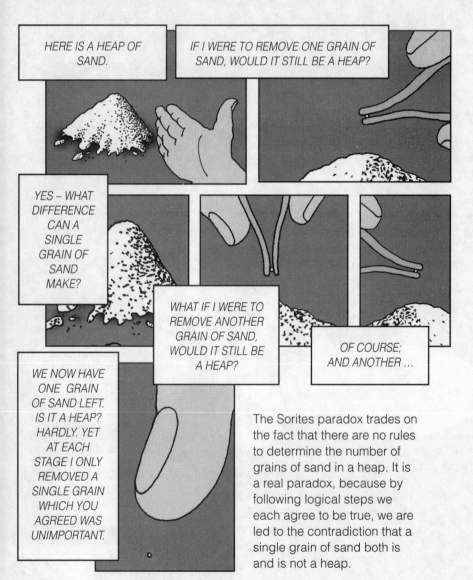

HERE IS A HEAP OF SAND.

IF I WERE TO REMOVE ONE GRAIN OF SAND, WOULD IT STILL BE A HEAP?

YES – WHAT DIFFERENCE CAN A SINGLE GRAIN OF SAND MAKE?

WHAT IF I WERE TO REMOVE ANOTHER GRAIN OF SAND, WOULD IT STILL BE A HEAP?

OF COURSE; AND ANOTHER ...

WE NOW HAVE ONE GRAIN OF SAND LEFT. IS IT A HEAP? HARDLY. YET AT EACH STAGE I ONLY REMOVED A SINGLE GRAIN WHICH YOU AGREED WAS UNIMPORTANT.

The Sorites paradox trades on the fact that there are no rules to determine the number of grains of sand in a heap. It is a real paradox, because by following logical steps we each agree to be true, we are led to the contradiction that a single grain of sand both is and is not a heap.

The Challenge to Sets

The Sorites paradox can be applied to more than just grains of sand. It can be applied to almost anything you can make minute changes to. Recently the philosopher Peter Unger published a paper called "I do not exist". There he performs a Sorites paradox on himself, removing one cell at a time. The Sorites has no bearing on formal logic, in which what matters is the pure manipulation of symbols. But once we try to apply meaning to those symbols, this paradox becomes very important, because many everyday words such as *few, a lot, big, small* and the like, as well as colours and sounds, may be used to generate a Sorites paradox.

PHILOSOPHERS GOT VERY EXCITED ABOUT COMBINING SETS AND LOGIC IN ORDER TO ANALYSE LANGUAGE. ONE COMMON IDEA IS THAT THE PREDICATES OF OUR LANGUAGE CORRESPOND TO SETS. SO THE PREDICATE "IS A HEAP" CORRESPONDS TO THE SET OF ALL HEAPS.

WHAT THE SORITES TELLS US IS THAT THERE WILL ALWAYS BE A QUESTIONABLE CASE ABOUT WHETHER SOMETHING IS A HEAP.

IF WE DO NOT HAVE A SOLUTION, THEN THE WHOLE ATTEMPT BECOMES VERY QUESTIONABLE.

Undermining Logic

Apart from threatening the attempt to use sets to analyse predicates of our language, the Sorites paradox throws into doubt the ability of Propositional and Predicate calculus to describe the way the world is.

> THE LAW OF IDENTITY (*a = a*) AND THE LAW OF NON-CONTRADICTION ¬(p&¬p) ARE TWO FUNDAMENTAL AXIOMS OF OUR SYSTEMS OF LOGIC. THE SORITES PARADOX CHALLENGES BOTH.

It challenges the law of identity because it seems to come up with the result that something that is a heap is also not a heap. For the same reason it also challenges the law of non-contradiction. Unsurprisingly, many contemporary philosophers and logicians have become rather upset by this result.

The Fiction of Vague Words

Many possible solutions have been offered. They broadly fall into three categories. Some suggest that the problem lies with applying vague concepts to the world. Others think that the vagueness is only apparent. A few think that the best thing to do is break away from the constraints of propositional and predicate logic. Frege thought that there should be no vague terms in logical argument. For Frege, the business of logic was scientific precision, and vague words serve only as a useful fiction in everyday speech.

Odysseus is wise

Patrick Stewart is bald.

WE UNDERSTAND BOTH "ODYSSEUS IS WISE" AND "PATRICK STEWART IS BALD". BUT JUST AS THERE IS NO ODYSSEUS, SO THERE IS NO PROPERTY OF BALDNESS.

IN MY PRECISE LANGUAGE, WE HAVE TO SET ASIDE BEARERLESS NAMES, AND SIMILARLY WE HAVE TO SET ASIDE PREDICATES THAT FAIL TO ATTRIBUTE EXPLICIT PROPERTIES.

Peter Unger's suggestion amounts to the fact that words like "people" are also such useful fictions.

What Do Words "Mean"?

Other contemporary thinkers opt to deny vagueness, or claim that the vagueness is only due to a lack of knowledge. They would claim, for example, that a particular number of grains of sand makes up a heap, but we may not know what it is. They believe that there is a genuine fact of the matter as to whether something is or is not a heap.

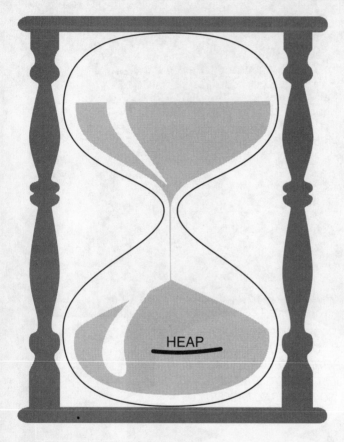

HEAP

So the good old laws of logic are in fact true of the world. The problem lies only with the words and concepts we use to talk about the world.

This solution to the Sorites paradox suggests that we do not really know what our words mean, since it is accepted that knowing what a word means involves knowing how to apply it correctly. But the solution explicitly denies that we have this sort of knowledge.

Fuzzy Logic

Because none of these solutions is conclusive or unproblematic, there are thinkers who have bitten the bullet and accepted the result of the paradox. They renounce the age-old demand that statements have one of two possible truth values: *true* or *false*. Now we can think of sentences as being "very true", "fairly true", "reasonably false", "completely false" and so on. Thus a whole family of logics is created, known collectively as "fuzzy logic".

THIS HAS THE ADDED ADVANTAGE OF ALLOWING US TO DEAL IN COMPARATIVE TRUTH VALUES. CONSIDER THESE SHAPES ...

IT IS TRUER TO SAY OF THE OVAL THAT "*IT IS ROUND*" THAN IT IS TO SAY IT OF THE RECTANGLE, DESPITE THE FACT THAT NEITHER IS REALLY ROUND.

With some fuzzy logic, truth may be thought of as a continuous scale:

100%		50%			0%
Completely true	Very true	Fairly true	Fairly false	Very false	Completely false

Fuzzy Heaps

Resorting to fuzzy logic is not a solution but a submission to the paradox. But even if we accept it, we cannot rid ourselves completely of the Sorites. The truth continuum of fuzzy logic lends itself to a version of the Sorites paradox.

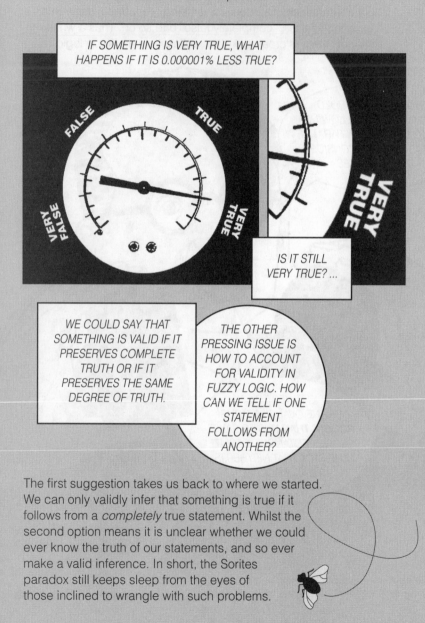

IF SOMETHING IS VERY TRUE, WHAT HAPPENS IF IT IS 0.000001% LESS TRUE?

IS IT STILL VERY TRUE? ...

WE COULD SAY THAT SOMETHING IS VALID IF IT PRESERVES COMPLETE TRUTH OR IF IT PRESERVES THE SAME DEGREE OF TRUTH.

THE OTHER PRESSING ISSUE IS HOW TO ACCOUNT FOR VALIDITY IN FUZZY LOGIC. HOW CAN WE TELL IF ONE STATEMENT FOLLOWS FROM ANOTHER?

The first suggestion takes us back to where we started. We can only validly infer that something is true if it follows from a *completely* true statement. Whilst the second option means it is unclear whether we could ever know the truth of our statements, and so ever make a valid inference. In short, the Sorites paradox still keeps sleep from the eyes of those inclined to wrangle with such problems.

Can Logic Escape Paradox?

The history of logic is littered with paradoxes. It may be seen as a struggle between two camps – the system-builders and the authors of paradox. For the most part, the system-builders are looking for precise ways to analyse our concepts. To do that, they try to use logic to derive all true statements in a clear and precise way. In contrast, a good paradox will challenge logic's ability to do this by casting doubt on our ability to distinguish or derive true and false statements or to provide clear definitions for our concepts.

TODAY'S SYSTEMS, DESPITE THEIR TECHNICAL INGENUITY, ARE ALMOST AS BESET BY PARADOXES AS THE LOGIC OF ANCIENT GREECE.

FOR WHILST PREDICATE CALCULUS IS ITSELF FREE OF PARADOXES, THE MOMENT WE TRY TO USE IT TO ANSWER QUESTIONS ABOUT THE WORLD, WE SOON RUN INTO TROUBLE.

Given these limitations of predicate calculus, it was only a matter of time before some logicians tried to move away from it and develop new systems of logic. Fuzzy logic is but one of these "non-classical" logics.

Non-Classical Logics: Intuitionism

One of the first alternatives to what is now called "classical logic" came from **L.E.J. Brouwer** (1881–1966). He objected to Frege and Russell's project of reducing mathematics to logic. He thought that mathematics rests on basic "intuitions" we have of what certain basic mathematical objects (like number and line) are. His view is hence known as "**intuitionism**".

The Devil's Argument

Brouwer concentrated mainly on cases of infinite sets and sequences. For example, the set of all positive numbers and the sequence of digits comprising irrational numbers like π and √2. Brouwer's argument could be put like this ...

I can *logically* prove to you that the sequence 666 must appear somewhere in the extension of any irrational number like π. For to say that it's not there, is the same as saying that for all digits of π, it is not the case that the sequence 666 appears in them. But that can never be *mathematically* proved. Even if you fill every piece of paper in the world with digits of π, there would still be infinitely more digits that you haven't checked.

Intuitionistic Logic

Although Brouwer wanted to show that some mathematical proofs work differently than logic, it was noticed that Brouwer's argument could also show that some branches of mathematics work according to a different logic. Some even developed such a logic and tried to show that it is in fact the logic of all mathematics. They called it "intuitionistic logic".

THE MAIN THING ABOUT INTUITIONISTIC LOGIC IS THAT IT DOESN'T INCLUDE THE RULE $\neg\neg p = p$, UNLESS THERE IS A CLEAR METHOD OF CHECKING WHETHER $\neg\neg p$ IS TRUE.

INFINITE SETS

FINITE SETS

$\neg\neg p = p$

THIS ALLOWS US TO USE THIS RULE IN CASES OF FINITE SETS, FOR EXAMPLE, BUT KEEPS OUT THE CASE OF INFINITE SETS AND SEQUENCES.

Intuitionism versus the *Reductio* Method

An important feature of intuitionistic logic is that in it Leibniz's *reductio* method cannot work. In the *reductio* method, we prove a mathematical statement by assuming its opposite and getting to a contradiction. But the move from "its negation is false" to "it is true" relies on the law of excluded middle. The *reductio* method doesn't give us a construction of the mathematical sentence from the axioms of some branch of mathematics, as mathematics is supposed to work.

WITHOUT GIVING US THE PROPER PROOF OF THE SENTENCE, YOU WANT TO SHOW IT MUST BE TRUE BECAUSE ITS NEGATION IS FALSE. SAYING THAT RELIES ON THE LAW THAT $\neg\neg p = p$, WHICH DOESN'T EXIST IN MY LOGIC.

THE PROBLEM IS THAT MANY FUNDAMENTAL MATHEMATICAL STATEMENTS – THAT EVERYONE WANTS TO ACCEPT – HAVE ONLY EVER BEEN PROVED USING MY **REDUCTIO** METHOD.

Excluded middle

The Intuitionistic Fad

This problem led to a new mathematical fad during the 1930s, of trying to find proofs to some basic and frequently used mathematical sentences using intuitionistic logic. Many such proofs were found. Departments of mathematics and philosophy were born and new academic divisions formed. Even Hilbert's formal methods, though being rivals to intuitionistic logic, were designed to use only approved intuitionistic procedures.

Until eventually, Gödel got interested.

USING HILBERT'S METHODS, I SHOWED THAT CLASSICAL FORMAL ARITHMETIC IS CONSISTENT IF AN INTUITIONISTIC ONE IS.

SO AS FAR AS CONSISTENCY IS THE MEASURE FOR MATHEMATICAL SYSTEMS, INTUITIONISTIC ONES ARE NOT SIGNIFICANTLY DIFFERENT FROM CLASSICAL ONES.

Interest in the debate has gone down a bit since then, but the basic notion – that we require a constructive proof to be sure a statement is true – still has its modern supporters among logicians, mathematicians, scientists and philosophers.

Addressing Some Old Problems

At around the same time, interest was sparked in an idea that a Polish mathematician named **Jan Lukasiewicz** (1897–1956) published in 1920. It did not stir much response outside Poland for over a decade. Lukasiewicz addressed some old problems that were known to exist in logic from Aristotle to Russell.

I ALREADY NOTICED THAT LOGIC IS ILL-EQUIPPED TO DEAL WITH SUCH WORDS AS "POSSIBLE" AND "NECESSARY", AND WITH STATEMENTS ABOUT THE FUTURE.

*HOW CAN WE DECIDE, AFTER ALL, WHAT THE TRUTH VALUE OF **"IT WILL SNOW ON BIG BEN IN A THOUSAND YEARS' TIME"** IS?*

97

The Value of Possible

Lukasiewicz wanted a logical system that could incorporate and deal with these elements of language. To do that, he designed a logic which had three truth values: false, true, and one that he thought of as "possible". Any statement in Lukasiewicz's logic can have the third truth value, as well as be false or true.

BECAUSE OF THAT, I HAD TO DECIDE NEW RULES FOR ALL THE LOGICAL CONNECTIVES. WHAT, FOR EXAMPLE, IS THE TRUTH VALUE OF **p&q** WHEN **p** IS TRUE AND **q** IS **POSSIBLE**?

TRUE   POSSIBLE   FALSE

p   q

Truth Values as Numbers

To solve this problem, it's easier to think of truth values as numbers. True and false have also been frequently represented as 1 and 0.

I DECIDED TO TREAT THE THIRD TRUTH VALUE AS THOUGH IT WAS $1/2$.

Using numbers, the truth value of **p&q** would be the smallest between the truth values of **p** and **q**.

Thus, if **p** is 1 and **q** is $1/2$, then **p&q** is also $1/2$.

The value of **pvq** is similarly the biggest among the truth values of **p** and **q**, so that if **p** is 0 and **q** is $1/2$ then the value of **pvq** would also be $1/2$.

The value of **¬p** would be 1 minus (the value of **p**), so that if **p** is possible ($1/2$), its negation is also possible.

The Possible and Non-Contradiction

As a result, in Lukasiewicz's logic neither the law of excluded middle nor the law of non-contradiction works. It is false to say that either **p** is true or **not-p** is true, for **p** can also be "possible". For the same reason, it is also false to say that **p** and ¬**p** cannot have the same truth value.

HOWEVER, THE LAW OF NON-CONTRADICTION WORKS IN MY LOGIC IN A DIFFERENT WAY.

IT MIGHT BE PUT LIKE THIS:

If p is true, then ¬p cannot also be true, and vice versa.

SO FUNNILY ENOUGH, IT CAN BE PROVED IN MY LOGIC THAT...

$$\neg\neg p = p$$

... WHICH WORKS WELL FOR ALL TRUTH VALUES OF **p**. IN THIS SENSE, IT IS VERY DIFFERENT FROM BROUWER'S LOGIC.

Despite the fact that two fundamental rules of classical logic do not apply in Lukasiewicz's logic, it is perfectly consistent and can be used just as well as Russell's logic. When the usual suspects became aware of Lukasiewicz's invention, it was quickly shown that his definitions of logical connectives could apply to create logics with any number of truth values from three to infinity.

All you need to do if you want, for example, to have a logic with 7 truth values is to give each truth value the numerical value of $\frac{1}{6}$. You'll have the truth values ...

$$0 \quad \frac{1}{6} \quad \frac{2}{6} \quad \frac{3}{6} \quad \frac{4}{6} \quad \frac{5}{6} \quad \frac{6}{6}$$

$$\left(\frac{1}{2}\right) \qquad\qquad (1)$$

i.e., seven truth values in total.

IT IS ENTIRELY UP TO YOU TO DECIDE WHAT THESE VALUES MEAN.

AS FAR AS LOGIC IS CONCERNED, LUKASIEWICZ'S RULES FOR LOGICAL CONNECTIVES WILL WORK PERFECTLY.

101

From Classical to Fuzzy Logic

Brouwer and Lukasiewicz initiated the modern period in logic.
Logic has evolved rapidly ever since. Now we have dozens of
systems of logic that are of interest to someone somewhere.
Logic was analysed into its simplest parts using tools that came
from algebra, and then put
together again to please any
taste and fashion.
Everything that happened
in logic from Aristotle to the
1930s was put in a single
package – *classical logic*.

*WITH LUKASIEWICZ,
"MANY-VALUED LOGIC"
WAS BORN, WHICH HAS
RECENTLY ALSO EARNED THE
MORE FUNKY NAME OF
"FUZZY LOGIC".*

*LUKASIEWICZ'S
ORIGINAL IDEA TO USE
HIS LOGIC TO DEAL WITH THE
WORD "POSSIBLE" DID NOT
CATCH ON, BUT MANY OTHER
APPLICATIONS WERE LATER
FOUND FOR FUZZY
LOGIC.*

Electronic "Possible" States

One important application of fuzzy logic is in the field of electronic machines. Remember the way many electronic devices work. These are typically devices that use **yes/no** or **on/off** switches, modelled on propositional calculus with the traditional two truth values, **true** and **false**. But there are machines that might use switches with more than two possible positions.

*THE KEYS IN THIS KEYBOARD ARE SIMPLY **ON/OFF** SWITCHES. IF I PRESS ONE, A SOUND COMES OUT.*

THIS OTHER ONE IS MUCH BETTER, WITH KEYS THAT HAVE MORE THAN TWO POSSIBLE STATES. THE SOUND THEY MAKE CHANGES AND BECOMES LOUDER THE HARDER I PRESS THEM, LIKE A REAL PIANO.

When machines use switches with more than two possible states, they can be modelled using fuzzy logic, just as easily as simpler ones can be modelled with propositional calculus.

The Fuzzy Logic Search Engine

Another important implication of fuzzy logic is in the field of AI. Suppose we want a smart information retrieval system, like an improved Web search engine. The more an engine can recognize what you are looking for from the list of words you give it, the better it will be.

> IF WE USE CLASSICAL PROPOSITIONAL CALCULUS IN OUR SEARCH ENGINE, THEN SITES EITHER MATCH THE WORDS YOU GIVE THE ENGINE OR THEY DON'T. EVERY SMALL VARIATION IN SPELLING COUNTS AS A NON-MATCH.

You searched for: Leonardo da Vinci

RESULTS:
Leonardo da Vinci
LEONARDO DA VINCI
da Vinci, Leonardo, Artist
Leonardo, Renaissance Master
The works of Leonardo da Vinci
Leonardo DiCaprio, actor
Leonard Cohen
Da Vinci's Drawings
The Mona Lisa, Leonardo's masterpiece
The helicopter, da Vinci's ideas
The inventions of the Renaissance –
Leo

> IF, HOWEVER, WE USE FUZZY LOGIC, THE ENGINE CAN FIND SITES MATCHING THE WORDS YOU GIVE TO VARYING DEGREES, AND BRING YOU MORE OF THE INFORMATION YOU NEED.

The Fuzzy Logical Machine

In general, fuzzy logic is a better tool than classical logic when it comes to pattern recognition, rather than finding 100% matches between things. Using fuzzy logic, we can get machines that tell when one thing is similar to another. This is an important skill with many applications in AI, such as word recognition, object recognition and so on.

Logic in the Quantum World

The 20th-century marriage of logic and algebra led to some other strange logics with important scientific and technological applications.

IN THE 1920s I HAD TO INVENT A SPECIAL MATHEMATICAL TOOL TO EXPRESS THE PHYSICAL BEHAVIOUR OF PARTICLES LIKE ELECTRONS IN QUANTUM MECHANICS. THE QUANTUM WORLD IS A VERY STRANGE WORLD AND NEEDS JUST AS STRANGE MATHEMATICAL MODELS TO DESCRIBE IT.

*SEVERAL DECADES LATER, MATHEMATICIANS FOUND AN ALGEBRAIC FORMULATION OF THE SPECIALLY DESIGNED "**HILBERT SPACES**".*

By then algebra and logic were so close that if we had an algebraic formulation of quantum mechanics, we could also have a logical one.

The Distributive Law of Quantum Logic

Quantum logic emerged in the 1960s. The idea is that the quantum universe – which scientists still find hard to understand and describe – works according to a logic of its own. As the philosopher **Hilary Putnam** (b.1926) said, this logic is very different from classical logic which comes from human language and reasoning.

*IN QUANTUM LOGIC THERE ARE TWO POSSIBLE TRUTH VALUES TO ANY SENTENCE, AS IN CLASSICAL LOGIC. THE MAIN DIFFERENCE BETWEEN CLASSICAL AND QUANTUM LOGIC CONCERNS THE **DISTRIBUTIVE LAW**, RATHER THAN ANY OF THE FUNDAMENTAL LAWS OF LOGIC LIKE THE EXCLUDED MIDDLE OR NON-CONTRADICTION.*

THE DISTRIBUTIVE LAW OF LOGIC STATES THAT

$$p \& (q \lor r) = (p \& q) \lor (p \& r).$$

How Quantum Logic Works

The distributive law of classical logic works like this ...

GIVE ME A PIECE OF CHOCOLATE CAKE, PLEASE.

WE HAVE CHOCOLATE CAKE WITH EITHER CHERRIES OR ALMONDS.

YOU MEAN YOU HAVE CHOCOLATE CAKE WITH CHERRIES, OR CHOCOLATE CAKE WITH ALMONDS.

In quantum logic this simple rule does not work.

The baker would still somehow have chocolate cake with either cherries or almonds, but when you check, you may find neither chocolate cake with cherries nor chocolate cake with almonds.

Confused? Now you know why physicists are going on about it so much.

Logic by Experiment

The invention of quantum logic has led Putnam to claim that the question which logic applies to the world is an *empirical* one and can only be answered by experiment. Putnam claimed that quantum mechanics is really the discovery that the subatomic world works according to a different logic than the one we are used to in the everyday world. Since then, Putnam had to rethink a little.

*I BECAME AWARE THAT TO BE ABLE TO READ THE RESULTS OF AN EXPERIMENT AND KNOW WHICH LOGIC IT SUPPORTS, WE MUST **ALREADY START** WITH SOME KIND OF REASONING. SO NOT ALL LOGIC IS GAINED FROM OBSERVATION.*

Classical Logic

Fuzzy Logic

I STILL BELIEVE THAT THERE ARE FACTS IN THE WORLD THAT DETERMINE WHICH LOGIC IT IS APPROPRIATE TO USE IN EACH CASE, AND THAT NO LOGIC IS BETTER THAN ANOTHER.

Quantum Logic

Quantum logic may not destroy the whole basis behind our belief in human reasoning, but it has applications that take us almost into the realms of science fiction.

1 TRUE   0 FALSE

SCIENTISTS TODAY HAVE SOME SUCCESS IN USING SINGLE ATOMS AS DIGITAL BITS. THEY CAN EXIST IN ONE OF TWO STATES, AND THERE'S NO HARM IN TAKING THESE STATES TO REPRESENT 1 AND 0, OR **TRUE** AND **FALSE**. THIS IS OF COURSE THE ULTIMATE VISION IN TERMS OF MINIMIZATION, SPEED AND EFFICIENCY.

The way we understand the world today, if we compute using single atoms, we are using tiny quantum computers. The logic that will be the best model for the actions of such computers would likewise be quantum logic. Although this is technology at its birth, there may soon come a day when many of our most complicated calculations will happen by the weird laws of quantum logic.

Logic and Science

If the only applications of logic were argument and the foundation of mathematics, then it would be a rather limited tool. However, the whole of modern science involves the application of logical and mathematical tools. Frege's logic was in fact designed to help create a rigorous scientific language. But the links between logic and science go back much further than that.

I DID NOT THINK MUCH OF MATHEMATICS, SO MY SCIENCE DID NOT RELY ON PRECISE MEASUREMENT OR EXPERIMENTATION. I CONCLUDED THAT HEAVENLY BODIES MOVE IN CIRCLES OUT OF THEIR LOVE OF GOD.

Unfortunately, trying to predict the motion of the planets using this idea proved very difficult. Eventually in the 2nd century AD, Ptolemy started to add more circles to Aristotle's system to account for the movement of mass.

The Copernican Revolution

Ptolemy's additions helped matters for a while, but Mars kept running out of its predicted orbit. This was dealt with by adding an ever increasing number of circles, until the Copernican revolution in the middle of the 15th century. Copernicus suggested predictions would be simplified if the earth went in circles around the sun.

THE CHURCH HAD ALREADY GIVEN ITS APPROVAL TO THE ARISTOTELIAN SYSTEM. MY SUGGESTION OFFENDED AGAINST THE INFALLIBILITY OF THE POPE.

Copernicus's heresy inspired people like Galileo and Kepler. Galileo thought that the controversy should be resolved by experiment. Using a brilliant bit of deduction, he concluded that if the earth moved round the sun, it would affect the motion of a pendulum. It does.

Galileo's Revolution

Galileo insisted that the phenomena of nature must be subject to careful observation and rigorous measurement. We should not rely on the authority of the past but on quantified observation. For him, "mathematics is the language of nature". Galileo revived Plato's idea that nature is governed by mathematical laws.

I DISCOVERED MY LAWS OF MOTION BY LOOKING AT THE MATHEMATICAL REGULARITIES IN EXPERIMENTS.

HIS RESULTS FORM THE EARLIEST START TO NEWTONIAN MECHANICS.

Galileo was forced to retract by the Church and spent the rest of his life in seclusion. But the cries of scientific revolution were beyond stopping now. Soon the Aristotelian world came tumbling down on itself.

Methods of Deduction and Induction

Galileo's methods became the methodology of science developed by the philosophers **Francis Bacon** (1561–1626) and René Descartes.

IN SCIENCE, FIRST WE PERFORM EXPERIMENTS, THEN WE GENERALIZE FROM THE EXPERIMENTAL RESULTS TO ARRIVE AT NATURAL LAWS.

ONCE WE HAVE THESE LAWS, WE CAN DEDUCE FROM THEM TO SEE WHAT SHOULD HAPPEN. WE CAN THEN PERFORM THE EXPERIMENT TO SEE IF THE PREDICTION IS RIGHT.

Descartes and Bacon represent two forms of reasoning – *deduction* and *induction*. Deduction is the method used to show that one theory follows from another. Induction is the method of inferring a general rule from a few cases.

INDUCTIVE REASON

THIS RAVEN IS BLACK.
THAT RAVEN IS BLACK …
ALL RAVENS ARE BLACK.

ALL RAVENS ARE BLACK.
THAT IS A RAVEN.
THEREFORE IT IS BLACK.

DEDUCTIVE REASON

Problems with Induction

In deduction, the truth of the conclusion follows from the truth of the premise. In an induction we can say no such thing. The fact that the two ravens are black does not contradict the fact that there is a white raven in Japan. But the general rule that "all ravens are black" is inconsistent with the existence of a white raven.

THEREFORE THE TRUTH OF THE SUPPORTING CLAIMS DOES NOT LOGICALLY GUARANTEE THE TRUTH OF THE CONCLUSION.

THIS POSES A PROBLEM FOR THE USE OF INDUCTION IN SCIENCE TO PRODUCE A GUARANTEED RESULT.

Hume's Fork

Although we are able to use induction with considerable success, nevertheless its application is questionable. The Scottish philosopher **David Hume** (1711–76) has been credited with the idea that our use of induction is unjustifiable.

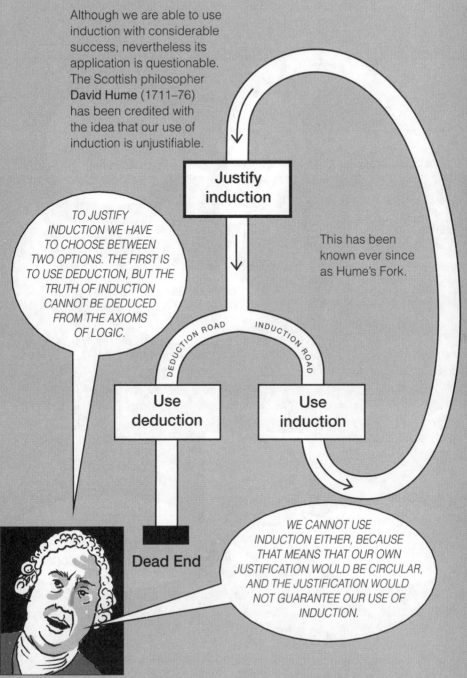

Justify induction

TO JUSTIFY INDUCTION WE HAVE TO CHOOSE BETWEEN TWO OPTIONS. THE FIRST IS TO USE DEDUCTION, BUT THE TRUTH OF INDUCTION CANNOT BE DEDUCED FROM THE AXIOMS OF LOGIC.

This has been known ever since as Hume's Fork.

DEDUCTION ROAD

INDUCTION ROAD

Use deduction

Use induction

Dead End

WE CANNOT USE INDUCTION EITHER, BECAUSE THAT MEANS THAT OUR OWN JUSTIFICATION WOULD BE CIRCULAR, AND THE JUSTIFICATION WOULD NOT GUARANTEE OUR USE OF INDUCTION.

Nomological Deduction

Hume thought that inductive inference is a *psychological fact* about human beings. Once we have been burnt, we will avoid putting our hand in the fire from then on. We "infer" by experience.

THIS IS EXACTLY THE PROBLEM. USING INDUCTION SEEMS TERRIBLY SENSIBLE.

BUT OUR USE OF IT CANNOT BE *JUSTIFIED*.

Attempts to ground our use of induction have not proved wholly conclusive. With the rise of the Vienna Circle, serious doubt was placed on the idea that science is truly inductive.

INSTEAD, THE IDEA OF "NOMOLOGICAL DEDUCTION" ROSE TO PROMINENCE.

THE IDEA IS THAT SCIENCE PROPOSES GENERAL LAWS FROM WHICH PARTICULAR RESULTS CAN BE DEDUCED.

Rather than believe that prediction and explanation require separate methodologies – one inductive and one deductive – we let deduction do all the work. We see a phenomenon, then come up with a law that may explain it causally. We then deduce what else follows from this law and seek empirical confirmation or falsification.

The nomological model began with the philosopher **John Stuart Mill** (1806–73). He thought that science was a division of logic and that inductive inferences were nothing but empirical generalizations. Confidence in these generalizations increases the more they are empirically confirmed as opposed to alternatives. But we are never completely certain of their conclusions. Common to all inductive inferences is the belief that everything in nature must have a cause or a condition that is both necessary and sufficient to cause its existence. We can discover both kinds by generalization from observation.

A NECESSARY CONDITION MUST BE FOUND ALONG WITH WHAT IT CAUSES ...

FOR EXAMPLE, CLOUDS ARE NECESSARY FOR RAIN. WE CAN FIND THIS OUT BY TRYING TO FIND CASES OF RAIN WITHOUT CLOUDS. IF WE CANNOT, THIS SUPPORTS THE CLAIM.

A sufficient condition is one that cannot exist without its effect – like fire with heat. Can we have a case of fire without heat?

Induction by Generalization

The work of the scientist is thus similar to the work of a chemist distilling some substance. By careful use of induction, deduction and elimination of candidates, the scientist eventually retains a few necessary and sufficient conditions for any phenomenon. The more experiments are made, the more the scientist can be sure of finding the correct causes for a certain effect.

INDUCTION

BYPASS

DEDUCTION ROAD

TION ROAD

Use
Deduction

I THOUGHT THAT MATHS AND LOGIC THEMSELVES ARE NOTHING BUT EMPIRICAL GENERALIZATIONS, REACHED BY USING A METHOD WE ARE VERY SURE OF.

EVERYTHING WE KNOW IS BY INDUCTION. SO, HUME'S FORK DOES NOT ARISE AS THE SPLIT BETWEEN INDUCTION AND DEDUCTION IS ERODED.

Hume claimed that we cannot use deduction to justify induction. But Mill argues that deduction itself is only thought to work because of *inducing generalizations* from our experience. Hume cannot use deductive reasoning to undermine induction because that form of reasoning itself rests on induction.

For Galileo, mathematics is the language of nature that can eventually discover the mathematical laws of nature. Mill instead considers maths another form of generalization. His idea is that science moves to ever more general rules that predict ever more accurately.

NEWTONIAN MECHANICS WAS A GREAT ACHIEVEMENT BECAUSE IT PREDICTED ALL MOVEMENTS AND FORCES WITH FOUR SIMPLE RULES.

> FROM THEM I COULD DERIVE ALL THE GREAT LAWS THAT PRECEDED ME – GALILEO'S LAW OF MOTION AND KEPLER'S ACCOUNT OF THE MOVEMENT OF THE PLANETS, FOR EXAMPLE.

Mill's view of mathematics and logic is quite original and unique. Mill thought that the certainty with which we hold mathematical and logical statements like $1+1=2$ and $\neg(p\&\neg p)$ is due to the huge number of empirical confirmations we have of them. Philosophers had for a long time tried to explain the supposedly necessary truth of mathematics and logic. Mill claimed that there is nothing to explain. These are not special statements but just more widely confirmed ones.

> THIS SHOT ALWAYS WORKED BEFORE.

Laws or Empirical Predictions

Philosophers have never been totally convinced by Mill's empirical justification for mathematics and logic. The problem is that the statements of mathematics – e.g., (2+2=4) – seem to behave as *laws*, not simply as *predictions* that, for example, if I put two and two apples together I will have four apples.

STRANGE, I HAD TWO APPLES IN THE BOWL, THEN ADDED TWO MORE, BUT NOW THERE ARE THREE APPLES THERE!

PERHAPS THIS IS A CASE WHERE YOUR GENERALIZATIONS FAIL YOU?

The rules of mathematics do not predict future events, but rather regulate what we take to be rational. Whenever we find a case that seems to falsify the rules of mathematics we always look for another rational explanation. There is just no case where we would give in and agree that the rules of maths are wrong in some cases.

It is also hard to see how such modern ideas as *imaginary numbers* and *geometry with more than three dimensions* can be generalizations from experience, since we never find these things in the real world.

The Raven Paradox

The deductive nomological method was modernized by **Karl Hempel** (1902–97) of the Vienna Circle. He described science as looking for general laws based on *causation* which would explain all and only the phenomena observed in experience. But he soon came to see problems with this model.

IF WE HAVE A GENERAL RULE OF THE FORM "ALL **F**s ARE **G**s" (ALL MEN ARE MORTAL), AND A STATEMENT OF THE FORM **Fa** (SOCRATES IS A MAN), THEN WE MAY CONCLUDE **Ga** (SOCRATES IS A MORTAL).

A LAW OF THIS FORM IS LOGICALLY EQUIVALENT TO THE LAW THAT ALL NON-**G**s ARE NOT **F** (EVERYTHING THAT IS IMMORTAL IS NOT A MAN).

If finding a man who is mortal confirms the law, then finding something that is not a man and is immortal also confirms the law. Armed with this, Hempel came up with a problem known as "the raven paradox"...

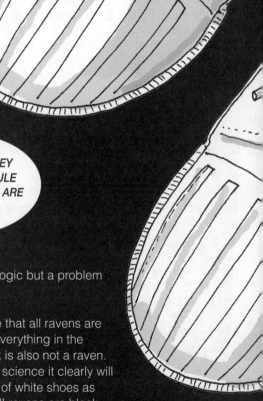

TAKE IT FROM ME THAT ALL RAVENS ARE BLACK! AND HERE IS THE PROOF ...

1:
ALL RAVENS ARE BLACK MEANS THAT ANYTHING THAT IS NOT BLACK IS NOT A RAVEN.

2:
NOW LOOK AT MY SHOES. THEY ARE NOT BLACK AND THEY ARE NOT RAVENS.

3:
THEREFORE, THEY CONFIRM THE RULE THAT ALL RAVENS ARE BLACK.

This is not a problem of logic but a problem posed by logic.

We could in theory prove that all ravens are black by checking that everything in the universe that is not black is also not a raven. But as a methodology of science it clearly will not do, for it takes a pair of white shoes as confirming the law that all ravens are black, as much as a black raven does. The problem is one of irrelevance: even if we knew that all tennis shoes are white we can see no way that this affects the colour of ravens.

A Problem of Cause and Effect

Another problem with Hempel's nomological account is that it does not distinguish between *cause* and *effect.* For example, the observation that a certain reading on a barometer is correlated with rain might equally well confirm the view that the presence of rain "causes" the reading of the barometer – or that the reading of the barometer "causes" the rain.

A GOOD SCIENTIFIC METHOD MUST TAKE ACCOUNT OF THE DIRECTION OF CAUSE AND EFFECT, BECAUSE NO ONE SERIOUSLY BELIEVES THAT BAROMETERS CAUSE RAIN.

WHAT WE HAVE HERE IS A CONJUNCTION OF TWO OBSERVATIONS: THE READING ON THE BAROMETER AND THE FACT THAT IT IS RAINING EQUALLY WELL CONFIRM THE FOLLOWING ARGUMENTS ...

1. Every time the barometer says that it is raining, it is raining.

2. The barometer says it is raining.

3. Therefore it is raining.

According to Hempel's proposed method, both explanations are equally possible as natural laws.

1. Every time it rains, the barometer says that it is raining.

2. It is raining.

3. Therefore the barometer says that it is raining.

Popper's Answer to Hempel

An idea of cause and effect is not enough to save the nomological model. Today almost no one believes in nomological deduction. The idea of the confirmation of a particular law by a particular observation has fallen by the wayside. One alternative suggestion came from Karl Popper.

LOGICALLY SPEAKING, TO SAY THAT IF F IS A NATURAL LAW, THEN G WILL HAPPEN, IS EQUIVALENT TO SAYING THAT IF G DID NOT HAPPEN THEN F IS NOT A NATURAL LAW. BUT IN TERMS OF OUR ABILITY TO CONFIRM THEM, THERE IS AN IMPORTANT DIFFERENCE.

THE FIRST FORMULATION REQUIRES US TO CHECK ALL Gs. THIS IS PRACTICALLY IMPOSSIBLE AS IT REQUIRES US TO CHECK EVERYTHING THAT HAS HAPPENED AND WILL EVER HAPPEN.

BUT A SINGLE CASE WHERE G HAS NOT HAPPENED IN RELEVANT CONDITIONS IS ENOUGH TO CONVINCE US THAT F IS NOT A LAW.

Popper went on to make this the basis of his scientific methodology. According to Popper, the proper way to do science is not to look for *confirmation* of our theories, but rather to try to *disconfirm* them.

By getting rid of the problem of confirmation, Popper thought the problem of induction was solved and science was based on solid logical ground.

Popper's Disconfirmation Theory

If a theory is disconfirmed in a particular case, then we reject it by a deduction very similar to the *reductio* method.

Popper's suggestion corresponds to the way that scientists actually work. Consider this example that ushered out Newtonian physics ...

ASSUME THAT NEWTONIAN PHYSICS IS TRUE. WE SHOULD THEREFORE BE ABLE TO DETECT LIGHT MOVING AT DIFFERENT SPEEDS.

When a theory is rejected, the race begins for a new theory that can account for all the results of the old theory and explain the new empirical data. If we end up with two theories that can account for the same data, then we should choose the simpler one.

The Probability of Viable Theory

Popper's disconfirmation or "falsifiability" theory displaces induction from its central role in the methodology of science. This means that all the worries about justification of induction and Hempel's worries about confirmation may be avoided.

As it is the job of a theory to account for all previous observations and make accurate predictions where previous theories failed, so a new theory also has to explain more. As science develops, its theories move away from common sense and become more and more improbable.

Theory 1

FACT FACT FACT FACT FACT

Theory 2

FACT FACT FACT FACT FACT FACT FACT FACT FACT FACT

A THEORY THAT EXPLAINS FIVE FACTS HAS A LARGER CHANCE OF BEING CORRECT THAN A THEORY THAT EXPLAINS TEN FACTS, SIMPLY BECAUSE IT DEALS WITH FEWER EVENTS THAT CAN BE FALSIFIED.

AS SCIENCE PROGRESSES AND THEORIES ACCOUNT FOR EVER MORE FACTS, SO THE PROBABILITY OF ITS THEORIES BEING CORRECT WILL DECREASE.

For a while, Popper's idea won a large number of converts, until **Willard Van Orman Quine** (1908–2000) published the paper "*Two Dogmas of Empiricism*" in 1951.

Popper's view was that an experimental result can falsify a particular scientific theory. For example, the observed orbit of the planet Mercury falsifies Newton's law of universal gravitation.

*SURELY THE OBSERVED ORBIT OF MERCURY CAN ONLY FALSIFY NEWTON'S THEORY IF THE **OBSERVATION** IS CORRECT ...*

*... IF WE GOT THE **LAWS OF OPTICS** CORRECT ...*

*... IF THERE IS NO **UNKNOWN INTERFERENCE** BETWEEN HERE AND MERCURY, AND SO ON AND SO FORTH.*

YES?

*SO INSTEAD OF **ONE** THEORY UNDER SUSPICION, YOU HAVE A HOST OF QUESTIONABLE ASSUMPTIONS. EACH ONE OF THEM COULD IN PRINCIPLE BE FALSIFIED BY EXPERIMENTAL DISCONFIRMATION. SO HOW DO YOU KNOW WHICH IS THE FALSE ONE?*

ERR??!!

Quine's "Web of Belief"

There is nothing in logic to say why, in Quine's view, we should reject Newtonian mechanics and not the laws of optics. When a collection of statements leads to a contradiction, at least one of them must be false, but logic does not tell us how to find out which. To say that the laws of optics have been observed time after time does not help, for it is logically possible that our faith in the measurements is misplaced.

TAKE THIS IDEA TO ITS EXTREME AND IT SAYS THAT ANY CASE OF "FALSIFICATION" POTENTIALLY THREATENS NOT ONLY THE THEORY IN QUESTION BUT ALSO OUR ENTIRE SET OF BELIEFS.

THERE IS NO WAY LOGICALLY TO DERIVE WHICH BELIEFS LEAD TO THE FALSE CONCLUSION.

Quine's criticism presents the question: how is our belief that "the countryside is pretty" to have any influence or bearing on the question of Newtonian mechanics?

ALL OUR BELIEFS ARE CONNECTED AND FORM A WHOLE. I CALL THIS THE "WEB OF BELIEF".

Quine thinks that the web only touches experience on the outside, but it is the web as a whole that is measured against experience.

Alterations to the "Web"

Changes to our certain beliefs at the heart of the web will have repercussions throughout the web, whilst changes to the softer outer regions will have less impact on the rest of the web. A major change will occur if our core beliefs are challenged – e.g., the conversion of St Paul to Christianity.

Quine states: *"The totality of our so-called knowledge or beliefs, from the most casual matters of geography and law to the profoundest laws of atomic physics or even pure mathematics and logic, is a manmade fabric which impinges on experience only along the edges ... A conflict with experience at the periphery occasions readjustments in the innermost part of the web."*

136

When any of our own beliefs faces a falsification by experience, it is the web as a whole that is challenged. According to Quine, we try to make as few alterations as possible to accommodate a new experience. So we try to change the soft parts of the web rather than the hard parts.

WE CHOSE TO REJECT NEWTONIAN MECHANICS RATHER THAN ANYTHING ELSE BECAUSE WE FOUND IT INVOLVED FEWER ALTERATIONS TO THE WEB AS A WHOLE.

$E=MC^2$

NONETHELESS, THE LAWS OF LOGIC ARE POTENTIALLY REVISABLE.

Insufficient Evidence

The result of this web of belief is that science is "underdetermined", which is to say that there is insufficient evidence to guarantee logically the truth of our scientific beliefs. This is because to derive the truth or falseness of any statement, we require a host of hidden premises effectively describing the whole of our web of belief. As Quine is at pain to emphasize, the web only touches experience at the *outside*. Experience teaches us very little, most of it is made up by us.

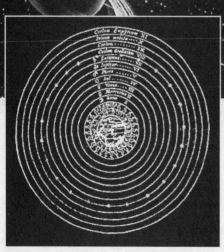

A SCIENTIFIC STATEMENT IS TAKEN TO BE TRUE IF IT CAN ACCOUNT FOR OUR EXPERIENCE WHILST MAKING MINIMAL CHANGES TO OUR WEB AS A WHOLE.

IF WE HAD A RADICALLY DIFFERENT WEB OF BELIEF, LIKE ARISTOTLE'S, THEN IT MIGHT BE THAT COMPLETELY DIFFERENT STATEMENTS WOULD DO THE JOB OF ACCOUNTING FOR AN EXPERIENCE WITH MINIMAL REPERCUSSIONS.

Even the basic question of what things there are in the world can only be answered in the light of the totality of our other beliefs.

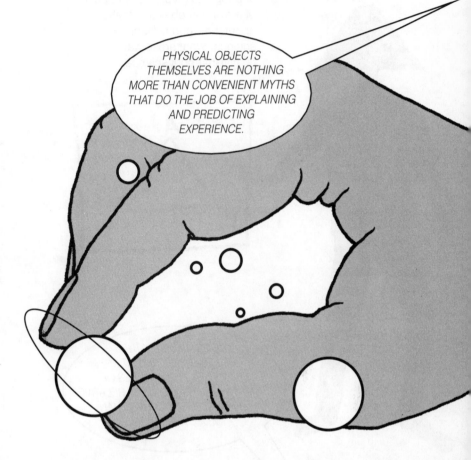

PHYSICAL OBJECTS THEMSELVES ARE NOTHING MORE THAN CONVENIENT MYTHS THAT DO THE JOB OF EXPLAINING AND PREDICTING EXPERIENCE.

"Physical objects are conceptually imported into the situation as convenient intermediaries – not by definition in terms of experience, but simply as irreducible posits comparable, epistemologically, to the gods of Homer. Let me interject that for my part I do, qua lay physicist, believe in physical objects and not in Homer's gods; and I consider it a scientific error to believe otherwise. But in point of epistemological footing the physical objects and the gods differ only in degree and not in kind."

Quine's Relativism

Quine's idea inspired a number of people to give up any hope of arriving at objective truths about the world through science. What arose was relativism about science.

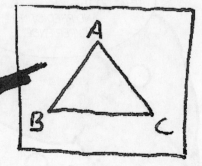

THE COMMON FEATURE OF RELATIVISM IS THAT IT PERCEIVES THE SUCCESS OF SCIENTIFIC THEORIES TO BE RELATIVE TO AN ELEMENT OTHER THAN OBJECTIVE TRUTH.

Quine's idea challenges the method of choosing between theories "in simplicity". What makes one theory simpler than the other? Instead of simplicity, philosophers have suggested that we choose between rival theories on grounds as diverse as politics and financial gain – or pragmatic advantages and aesthetic preference.

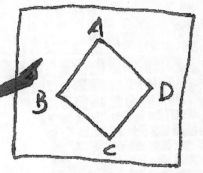

Feyerabend's Denial of Scientific Method

The most extreme form of this view was voiced by the "anarchist" philosopher of science **Paul Feyerabend** (1924–94) who denies the existence of any scientific method.

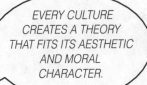

EVERY CULTURE CREATES A THEORY THAT FITS ITS AESTHETIC AND MORAL CHARACTER.

Davidson's Reply to Quine

Donald Davidson had significant doubts about rejecting scientific method. His opposition starts with Quine's belief that logic is in principle revisable.

IN ORDER TO KNOW HOW TO CHANGE OUR WEB, WE SHOULD BE ABLE TO TELL WHAT WOULD FOLLOW FROM A POSSIBLE CHANGE IN THE WEB.

HOW ELSE DO WE KNOW THAT OUR CHANGE WILL NOT CONFLICT WITH EXPERIENCE? IN SHORT, WE MUST HAVE SOME SORT OF **PROOF THEORY**.

This means that not only can we not avoid some sort of logic, but also that this proof theory cannot itself be revisable. For if we could change the method of proof, then we would have no way of telling what the consequences might be. So, at the very least, the web must have an unchangeable core.

The Presentation of Truth

Davidson's complaint with relativism goes further. If our web is genuinely to be a "web of belief", then we must assume that it aims at truth. To believe *something* and to believe that it is *true* amounts to the same thing. All webs must share a common ground of truth.

TRUTH IS NOT PART OF THE CHANGEABLE WEB, BUT PART OF ITS "HARD EDGES", SO TO SPEAK.

BECAUSE OF THIS, ALL WEBS MAY BE COMPARED WITH EACH OTHER IN TERMS OF TRUTH.

Davidson's elevation of truth along with logic to solid ground is hardly surprising, since logic is the study of the *presentation of the truth*.

Hard-edged Truth versus Relativism

Davidson embraces Quine's view that science is under-determined, but rejects Quine's totally revisable web. In its place comes a partially revisable web, hanging between a hard core of logic and the hard edges of truth. Truth provides a rigid base on which an ever-improving structure is built.

TRAPPED BETWEEN THE TWO OF THEM, THERE IS NO ROOM FOR US TO FIX OUR BELIEFS BY DISREGARDING THE FACTS.

DAVIDSON TELLS US THAT SCIENCE IS A WAY OF APPROXIMATING TRUTH. HOWEVER, HE OFFERS LITTLE BY WAY OF METHODS FOR APPROXIMATING THE TRUTH, NOR DOES HE OFFER A JUSTIFICATION FOR SCIENTIFIC METHOD. CONSEQUENTLY, HE FAILED TO CONVINCE HARDENED RELATIVISTS.

Cognitive Science and Logic

Aside from logic's importance to scientific methodology, there are sciences which make obvious use of logic and even aspire to being overtly logical. Such motivation comes from computers. Just as you could talk of computer programs knowing nothing whatsoever about the underlying electronics, so cognitive science hopes to understand human consciousness with no regard to the behaviour of a system of brain cells of which we know very little.

IN A COMPUTER, WE CAN GET AWAY WITH DISREGARDING THE ELECTRONICS BECAUSE WE CONSTRUCTED IT TO BEHAVE AS A LOGICAL SYSTEM.

THE COMMON ASSUMPTION OF THE COGNITIVE SCIENCES IS THAT THE MIND IS A SIMILAR LOGICAL SYSTEM.

Turing was a big supporter of this assumption. It motivated his repeated attempts to create the first digital computers. The boom of the cognitive sciences is for the most part due to the success of Turing's machines and the rise of Chomskian linguistics.

Chomsky's Universal Grammar

Noam Chomsky's (b.1928) interest in linguistics was directed to a central issue of language learning. At the time, it was thought that children learn language by imitating adults. Experiments showed that children can create grammatically correct sentences that they have never heard. A three-year-old will correct an adult's grammar but never argue with them over facts.

Determinator adjective noun verb noun phrase.

TO EXPLAIN THIS, I SUGGESTED THAT THERE MUST BE INNATE "UNIVERSAL GRAMMAR". EVERY CHILD IS BORN WITH CERTAIN GRAMMATICAL RULES HARDWIRED INTO THEIR BRAINS.

IN THE PROCESS OF LEARNING A LANGUAGE, A CHILD LEARNS NOT ONLY WORDS BUT WHERE THESE WORDS STAND IN RELATION TO ALREADY EXISTING GRAMMATICAL RULES.

Welsh
Slovak
Czech
Portuguese
English
French
Urdu
Hindi
Arabic

Vocabulary

Clause construction

Gender

Word order

Universal Grammar

According to Chomsky, this humanly innate universal grammar is rich enough to create all human languages. So all human languages are based on the same universal structure. The universal grammar contains several possible configurations which determine the grammar of any human language. These include *word order*, whether or not the language has *gendered* nouns and *verbs*, and how it constructs *clauses*.

Noun and Verb Categories

Our innate grammar divides words into different systematic categories. A child is born with these categories. As it learns the vocabulary of a language, it also learns in which category to place a word. These categories, along with a few simple rules of syntax, define how words may be combined to form sentences. The two most important categories are *nouns* and *verbs*.

A SENTENCE OF ANY LANGUAGE MAY BE DIVIDED INTO NOUN PHRASES AND VERB PHRASES. CONSIDER THIS SIMPLE SENTENCE: "*PIGS FLY.*" IT MAY BE DIVIDED AS FOLLOWS ...

Pigs fly.

Sentence

Noun phrase

Verb phrase

Noun

Verb

Pigs

fly

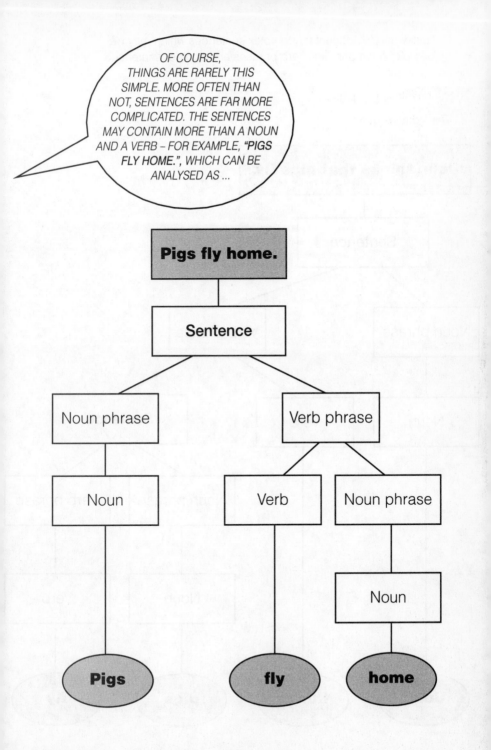

149

Chomsky had to account for complex sentences which may be made up of noun phrases, verb phrases and another sentence. For example ...

"John thinks that pigs fly."

This comes out as ...

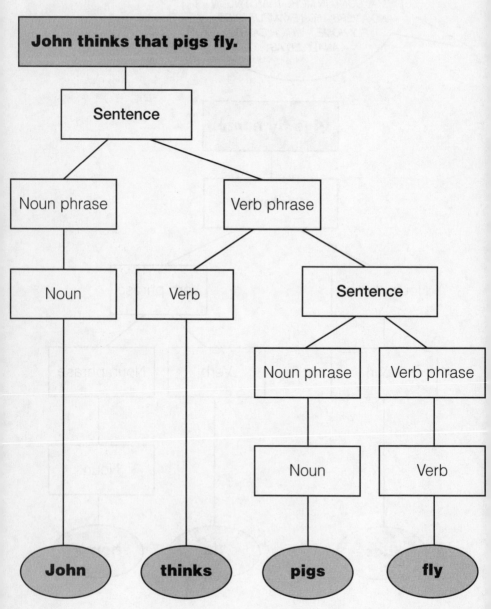

Recursive Rules of Grammar

The construction rules of universal grammar are *recursive*. "Recursive" means the repeated application of a rule, definition or procedure to successive results. Chomsky believed that this was the only way to account for sentences of potentially infinite length. But this was not enough. Language allows for a great variety of linguistic constructions, many of which require new rules of combination. Eventually, there became so many added rules that Chomsky required an underlying structure to support his theory.

UNIVERSAL RULES OF GRAMMAR

ACTUAL SENTENCES (INFINITE)

WHILE MORE AND MORE RULES ARE REQUIRED TO ACCOUNT FOR THE DIVERSITY OF LANGUAGE, ALL OF THESE NEW RULES SEEM TO FOLLOW THE SAME BASIC RECURSIVE PATTERN.

BY IDENTIFYING THIS PATTERN, WE CAN RELATE THEM ALL BACK TO A SINGLE, EVEN MORE ABSTRACT GRAMMAR.

The X-bar Theory

Chomsky claimed that a simple set of recursive rules can explain the formation of any grammatical phrase. He gave it the catchy name "x-bar" theory.

In x-bar theory, x and y stand for grammatical categories. X-bar and y-bar stand for the corresponding grammatical phrase. Their simple rule of formation is x-bar=x+y-bar. This is a simple formula of recursive application.

Let's take for example the phrase, "the clock in the corner".

ACCORDING TO X-BAR THEORY, IT IS CONSTRUCTED LIKE THIS ...

key:

n-bar	noun phrase
p-bar	preposition phrase
n	noun
p	preposition

A Logical Theory

Chomsky believed that x-bar theory can explain both the process of language learning and people's intuitive grasp of their native language. Supplemented with an appropriate mechanism for word order and transformation rules, Chomsky thought x-bar theory is sufficient to explain all grammatical constructions in any given language.

X-bar theory is a logical theory because it is concerned with form rather than content and with the construction of strings of symbols by successive application of a few simple rules.

I BELIEVE WE ARE BORN WITH A LANGUAGE MECHANISM IN THE BRAIN THAT CAN BE DESCRIBED AS A LOGICAL PROGRAM.

If Chomsky is right, then our understanding of natural language comes down to a computation based on our innate grammar.

Influenced by this idea, some prominent philosophers have proclaimed the brain to be in part little more than a complex computer negotiating language along Chomskian lines.

Problems of Syntax and Semantics

Chomskian linguistics goes some way towards thinking of natural language in "model-theoretic" terms. Chomsky himself is more concerned with syntax than semantics, but realizes that for languages such as English, syntax and semantics cannot be completely divorced.

Chomsky found that he had to look at the semantics of each word in order to explain why some sentences that seem to be syntactically well formed are in fact meaningless. For example:

"I cried

THIS LOOKS LIKE AN INNOCENT *SUBJECT-VERB-OBJECT* SENTENCE, BUT IT IS OBVIOUSLY SILLY.

WE CANNOT SAY THAT THIS FORM OF SENTENCE IS UNGRAMMATICAL, AS MOST SENTENCES OF THIS FORM ARE PERFECTLY FINE ...

... FOR EXAMPLE, *"I FIRED HER."*

her."

The difference between the grammatically correct and incorrect sentences must lie with the *meaning* of the verb.

FOR THIS REASON, I INTRODUCED A NUMBER OF CRITERIA TO DESCRIBE THE BEHAVIOUR OF WORDS.

THESE CRITERIA DETERMINE WHICH WORDS MAY BE COMBINED TO FORM SENTENCES IN MORE DETAIL THAN THE SIMPLE DISTINCTION BETWEEN NOUN PHRASES AND VERB PHRASES.

Chomsky suggests categories that describe whether the word is *active* or *passive*; whether it implies *intention* and so on. The rules governing the behaviour of these categories form part of a highly intricate semantic model that is still being refined.

155

Complex Grammatical Structures

Chomskian linguistics enjoyed a good deal of initial success in dealing with structured languages like English and French. But within these there are a number of dialects – e.g., Cockney rhyming slang and Parisian back slang – and additionally a large number of regional accents. Chomskian linguistics aspires to explain them all. To do this, it has been forced to add progressively more layers of grammatical structure.

Deep grammar
(x-bar theory)

A SIMPLE HIERARCHY WOULD LOOK A BIT LIKE THIS ...

Phonological form
(issues of pronunciation)

Logical form
(semantic issues
reflected in grammar,
e.g., *"I fired her"* is
grammatically
correct but *"I cried
her"* is not)

Surface grammar
(word order, etc.)

Each stage of Chomsky's hierarchy contains a huge
amount of information and its own set of recursive rules.
This structure runs along with other complex structures,
like the *vocabulary* of the language and word
morphology – the structure of the words themselves.

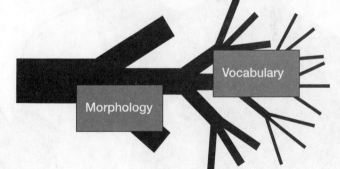

Vocabulary

Morphology

So large is the amount of information involved that it
seems improbable that human evolution could have
generated such a complex structure. This suggests the
question of whether there is enough space or structure
in the newborn's brain to contain all this information.

Problems with "Universal" Grammar

The assumption of universal grammar is further shaken when we move to examine languages other than the Western European ones, e.g., Slavonic, Semitic and aboriginal languages. In these languages, word order is of very little importance. While some meaningful structures are more common than others, very few are actually ungrammatical.

SOME OF US UNDERSTAND TIME TO BE CYCLICAL, WHICH EXPLAINS THE RELATIVE LACK OF TENSING IN OUR LANGUAGE.

OTHERS HAVE NO ABSTRACT NOUNS. OUR LANGUAGE SIMPLY MISSES OUT A CATEGORY OF WORDS THAT YOU TAKE TO BE INNATE.

The absence of abstract nouns in actual languages proves that languages can exist without them, which in turn casts doubt on whether we are all born with an innate grasp of them.

DESPITE THIS, WE STILL NEED SOME ACCOUNT OF THE SPEED AND ACCURACY WITH WHICH WE LEARN LANGUAGES. A FINITE SET OF AXIOMS IS A GOOD WAY TO ACCOUNT FOR THIS.

It must be remembered that generative linguistics is a relatively new science, so it is hardly surprising that theories must evolve to account for difficult cases. It is just that at present we have no better explanation.

The Symbolic Brain Model

Inspired by the success of Chomskian linguistics, many philosophers and psychologists aspire to explain all human mental life the way Chomsky tried to explain language. They conceive of the mind as the result of an immense number of logical manipulations in the brain. This program roughly divides into two camps, each employing two different logical systems. We can think of these as two models: the I-Robot and Y-Robot.

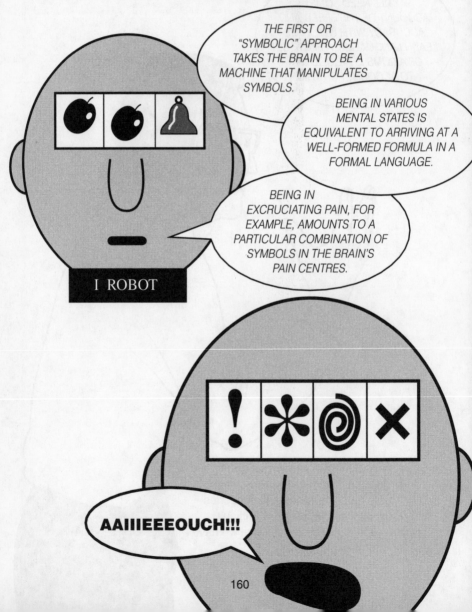

THE FIRST OR "SYMBOLIC" APPROACH TAKES THE BRAIN TO BE A MACHINE THAT MANIPULATES SYMBOLS.

BEING IN VARIOUS MENTAL STATES IS EQUIVALENT TO ARRIVING AT A WELL-FORMED FORMULA IN A FORMAL LANGUAGE.

BEING IN EXCRUCIATING PAIN, FOR EXAMPLE, AMOUNTS TO A PARTICULAR COMBINATION OF SYMBOLS IN THE BRAIN'S PAIN CENTRES.

I ROBOT

AAIIIEEEOUCH!!!

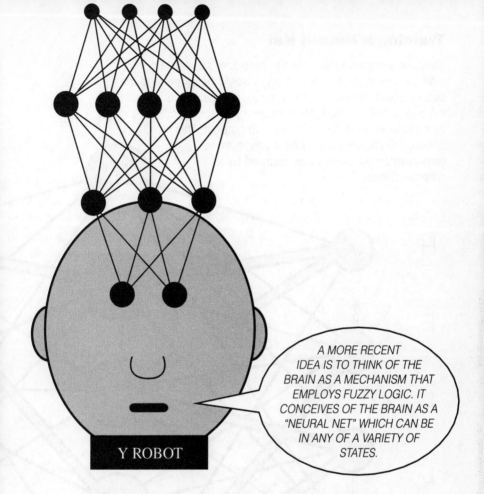

A MORE RECENT IDEA IS TO THINK OF THE BRAIN AS A MECHANISM THAT EMPLOYS FUZZY LOGIC. IT CONCEIVES OF THE BRAIN AS A "NEURAL NET" WHICH CAN BE IN ANY OF A VARIETY OF STATES.

Y ROBOT

A neural net is composed of units which behave like brain cells (neurones). Like a neurone, they are connected to multiple inputs and multiple outputs. The response is governed by the overall effect of the input received. The process of computation that goes on within the net is not akin to a formal deduction. The only way we have of modelling this behaviour is statistical, and as such we know very little about a particular net.

A simple neural net looks like this ...

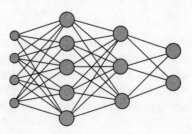

Training a Neural Net

Suppose we train a neural net to produce "spoken" English
words correctly from text. The input would be letters and the
output would be sound. The "neurones" have to learn to relate
the two correctly. The system learns by attaching different levels
of importance to different inputs and outputs. This is
done by multiplying each of the connections
(represented by lines in the diagram) by a
different number.

H

E

L

L

O

Initially, the connections are given small random
numbers. Then the results that the net gives are
corrected and a different weighting is tried. The
machine will continue to alter the weighting whilst
producing statistically improved results.

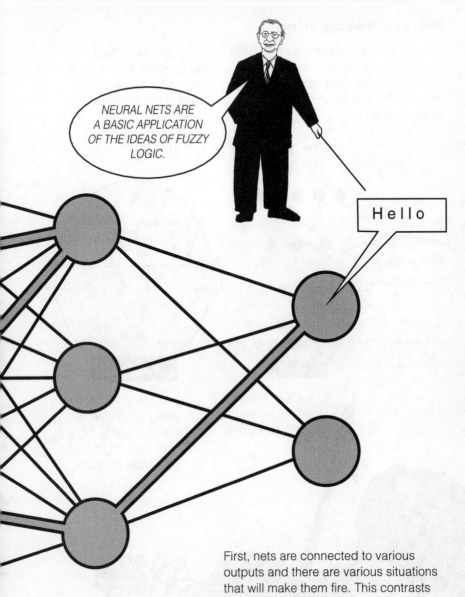

First, nets are connected to various outputs and there are various situations that will make them fire. This contrasts with the behaviour of a vending machine which is based on propositional calculus and only ever has one output for each state. Second, the different weightings given to the different connections are a numerical equivalent to the multiple truth values of fuzzy logic.

Pattern Recognition

Compared to digital computers, neural nets are particularly good at *pattern recognition*. This leads them to excel at producing word sounds from text where a conventional computer would flounder. There is no problem in getting a neural net to recognize a piece of music ...

... but it probably could not tell you what the notes are.

A digital computer could recognize the notes easily, but it is very hard to get it to recognize the style.

The human brain seems to behave in a similar way. Humans find it very easy to categorize things but spend many years learning how to do mathematics.

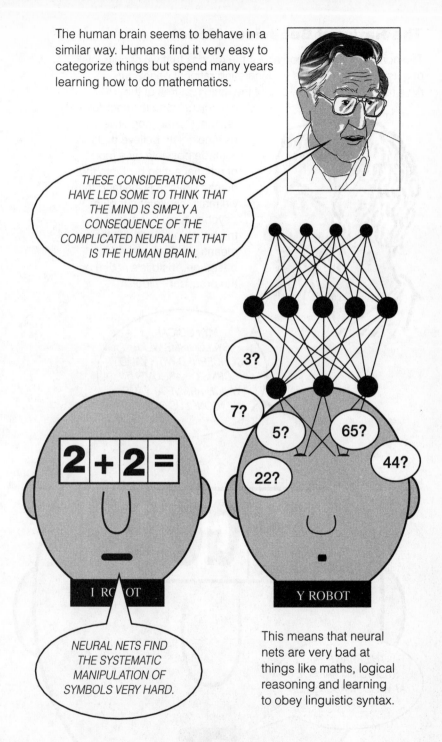

THESE CONSIDERATIONS HAVE LED SOME TO THINK THAT THE MIND IS SIMPLY A CONSEQUENCE OF THE COMPLICATED NEURAL NET THAT IS THE HUMAN BRAIN.

3?

7?

5?

65?

22?

44?

2 + 2 =

I ROBOT

Y ROBOT

NEURAL NETS FIND THE SYSTEMATIC MANIPULATION OF SYMBOLS VERY HARD.

This means that neural nets are very bad at things like maths, logical reasoning and learning to obey linguistic syntax.

The Rational Behaviour Model

The dominant assumption about the mind is that we should think of it as a model involved in generating rational behaviour. According to this theory, one of the main features of the conscious mind is to act *for* a reason. Certain cognitive psychologists believe that this is made possible by a model of rational action built into the human brain. It is claimed that we make sense of our own psychological behaviour and the behaviour of others by means of this model. It is based on Aristotle's notion of the practical syllogism ...

MY LOGICAL SYLLOGISMS WERE CONCERNED WITH VALID FORMS OF ARGUMENT WHICH ARRIVE AT VALID CONCLUSIONS.

GO GO GO

THE PRACTICAL SYLLOGISMS ARRIVE AT VALID REASONS FOR ACTION.

Practical Reason

In a practical syllogism, the first premise is a statement of desire, e.g., "I want to eat."

The second premise is a statement of belief, e.g., "There is food in my fridge."

These lead to a conclusion that recommends a course of action – "I should go to the fridge."

MANY COGNITIVE PSYCHOLOGISTS BELIEVE THAT OUR MIND IS EQUIPPED WITH A PICTURE OF THE WORLD CONTAINING MANY THINGS THAT WE TAKE TO BE TRUE.

It is also maintained that we contain some sort of "deliberation mechanism" that extracts goals from needs. These are then combined with the world picture to give reasons for action. This is called the "belief/desire" model.

What is Consciousness?

Although most cognitive psychologists and philosophers of mind hold this "practical" view, there is still much unresolved disagreement.

Whatever the differences, the fact remains that they all see the brain as a machine that follows rules of rational thinking. Our conscious life is the result of electro-chemical reactions in the brain that instantiate an immensely complex logical manipulation machine. Whether this is convincing or not, a lot of effort is going into cracking the computer program that is human consciousness.

The Place of Logic

Logic gets into all forms of human inquiry. All good arguments should be logical, so they must follow logical rules to show that the conclusions follow from the premises. Logic itself makes very few claims about anything. It is a tool, a method of analysis.

SO LOGIC DOES NOT DICTATE THAT THE GOOD OF THE MANY OUTWEIGHS THE GOOD OF THE FEW?

NO, LOGIC CANNOT MAKE SUCH CLAIMS. BUT IT DOES PROVIDE YOU WITH A WAY OF REACHING THAT CONCLUSION FROM CERTAIN PREMISES.

Logic can be used for more than that. The emphasis that modern logic puts on syntactic rules allows us to use it for everything from digital electronics to analysing language.

Wittgenstein's Change of View

Logic seems an inseparable part of our lives. But not everyone is convinced that logic is so vital. In his later period, Wittgenstein moved away from the faith in logic he held as a young man. In a famous dialogue with Turing, he was keen to press the practical consequences over theoretical worries. With scepticism about the role of logic came a new view of philosophy.

WITTGENSTEIN CAME TO THINK THAT WHAT WAS IMPORTANT IN PHILOSOPHY WAS NOT ARGUMENT BUT GETTING PEOPLE TO SEE THINGS FROM A NEW PERSPECTIVE.

WORK ON PHILOSOPHY IS – AS WORK IN ARCHITECTURE FREQUENTLY IS – ACTUALLY MORE A KIND OF WORK ON ONESELF. ON ONE'S OWN CONCEPTION. ON THE WAY ONE SEES THINGS.

If someone believes that he has found the solution to the "problem of life"… then in order to refute himself, he would only have to remember that there was a time when this "solution" had not been found; but at that time too one had to be able to live …

AND THAT IS WHAT HAPPENS TO US IN LOGIC.

IF THERE WERE A "SOLUTION" TO LOGICAL PROBLEMS, THEN WE WOULD ONLY HAVE TO CALL TO MIND THAT AT ONE TIME THEY HAD NOT BEEN SOLVED (AND THEN TOO ONE HAD TO BE ABLE TO LIVE AND THINK).

Perhaps unsurprisingly, coming at the end of a century in which logic has enjoyed such tangible success, very few are prepared to follow Wittgenstein in his line of thought. Instead, logic continues to play a part in forming the foundation of Western science, mathematics and technology.

WHETHER IT BELONGS TO THE ESSENCE OF THOUGHT AND LANGUAGE OR NOT, THE ABILITY TO THINK SYSTEMATICALLY AND TO PROVE THAT YOU ARE THINKING IN STEPS THAT FOLLOW ONE FROM THE OTHER, TURNS OUT TO BE A FORMAL ADVANTAGE WHEN APPLIED TO A GREAT VARIETY OF CONTENTS.

Further Reading

Greek Logic

Aristotle, "Prior Analytics", in J. Barnes (ed.), *The Complete Works of Aristotle*, Princeton University Press (1984). Aristotle's most developed account of his logic.

Barnes, J. (ed.), *The Cambridge Companion to Aristotle*, Cambridge University Press (1995). Contains articles on all aspects of Aristotle's philosophy, including an excellent article on his logic by R. Smith.

Gerson, L.P. and Inwood, B. (trans.), *Hellenistic Philosophy: Introductory Reading*, Hackett (1998). Contains translations on various pieces of post-Aristotelian philosophy, including a reasonable amount on Stoic logic.

Logic and Maths

Frege, G., *Begriffsschrift* (1879). A full translation can be found in J. van Heijenoort (ed.). Frege's account of his formal apparatus that paved the way for later developments but was surpassed by them.

—— *The Foundations of Arithmetic*, trans. J.L. Austin, Blackwell (1953). A highly regarded, non-formal account of Frege's views on the nature of numbers and also some of his key claims in the philosophy of language.

—— *The Basic Laws of Arithmetic*, trans. M. Furth, University of California Press (1964). A combination of the *Begriffsschrift* and *The Foundations of Arithmetic*.

Gödel, K., "On Formally Undecidable Propositions of Principia Mathematica and Related Systems", in *Kurt Gödel: Collected Works*, vol. 1, ed. S. Feferman, Oxford University Press (1990). Home of the incompleteness proof. Almost impossible to grasp without a significant quantity of symbolic logic.

van Heijenoort, J. (ed.), *From Frege to Gödel: A Source Book in Mathematical Logic, 1879–1931*, Harvard University Press (1967). This very useful collection contains key works by Frege, Hilbert, Brouwer and Gödel. Not for the beginner.

Hilbert, D., "On the Infinite", in J. van Heijenoort (ed.). A full account of Hilbert's views on the foundations of mathematics.

Kenny, A., *Frege*, Penguin (1995). Introduces Frege's major ideas in an easy-to-grasp way that requires no prior reading.

Nagel, E. and Newman, J.R., *Gödel's Proof*, Routledge (1959). A short, clear, easy introduction to the eponymous proof.

Russell, B. and Whitehead, A.N., *Principia Mathematica* (1910–13), second edition, Cambridge University Press (1994). A two-volume magnum opus giving a formal account of the foundations of arithmetic.

Russell, B., *Introduction to Mathematical Philosophy*, Allen and Unwin (1919), reprinted by Routledge (1993) with a new introduction. A shorter, less formal account of the foundations of arithmetic.

Logic and Language

Carnap, R., "Intellectual Autobiography", in Paul A. Schlipp (ed.), *The Philosophy of Rudolf Carnap*, Open Court Publishing (1963). Carnap sketches his own intellectual development in a relatively accessible way.

—— *The Logical Syntax of Language*, trans. Amethe Smeaton, Kegan Paul, Trench, Trubner & Co. (1937). A weighty tome developing Carnap's proposal.

Chomsky, N., *Generative Grammar: Its Basis, Development and Prospects*, Kyoto University of Foreign Studies (1988). Gives an early, and so less convoluted, account of the generative grammar system.

Davidson, D., *Inquiries into Truth and Interpretation*, Oxford University Press (1984). A collection of Davidson's papers connected with his views on language, including "Truth and Meaning" (1967) and "Radical Interpretation" (1973).

Heaton, J. and Groves, J., *Introducing Wittgenstein*, Icon Books (1999). One of the better accounts of both his early and late views in print, despite being a "mere" outline.

Maher, J. and Groves, J., *Introducing Chomsky*, Icon Books (1999). A reader-friendly outline of Chomsky's thought.

Neale, S., *Descriptions*, MIT Press (1990). Clear exposition and defence of Russell's theory of descriptions.

Russell, B., "On Denoting" (1905), reproduced in *Logic and Knowledge: Essays 1901–1950*, Allen and Unwin (1956). Classic article expounding the theory of descriptions. Covers much of the same ground as Russell's *Introduction to Mathematical Philosophy*, ch. XVI.

Wittgenstein, L., *Tractatus Logico-Philosophicus*, Routledge. Two translations are available: the first by C.K. Ogden (1922) was endorsed by Wittgenstein himself, while the second by D.F. Pears and B.F. McGuiness (1961) is generally preferred. One of the most difficult and rewarding books in 20th-century philosophy. Home of the picture theory and Truth Tables.

—— *Philosophical Investigations*, trans. G.E.M. Anscombe, Blackwell (1953). Brilliant, thought-provoking rejection of much that came before and that followed, including his earlier *Tractatus*.

Logic and Science

Davidson, D., "On the Very Idea of a Conceptual Scheme" (1974), reprinted in his *Inquiries into Truth and Interpretation*. An articulate assault on relativism.

Hume, D., *A Treatise of Human Nature* (1739), ed. D.F. Norton and M.J. Norton, Oxford University Press (2000). Another landmark in philosophy and the supposed origin of inductive scepticism.

Kuhn, T.S., *The Structure of Scientific Revolutions* (1962), second edition, University of Chicago Press (1970). A clear, well-argued, well-written case for relativism.

Popper, K., *Objective Knowledge: An Evolutionary Approach*, Clarendon Press (1972). Popper argues for the rejection of the idea that science needs induction.

Quine, W.V.O., "Two Dogmas of Empiricism" (1951), reprinted in his *From a Logical Point of View*, Harvard University Press (1953). A classic paper, the last section of which gives a short introduction to the web of belief.

Paradoxes

Sainsbury, M., *Paradoxes*, second edition, Cambridge University Press (1995).

Williamson, T., *Vagueness*, Routledge (1994). An entire book dedicated to sorites reasoning.

Textbooks

Larson, R. and Segal, G., *Knowledge of Meaning: An Introduction to Semantic Theory*, MIT Press (1995). Just about the closest thing there is to a textbook of formal semantic theory, as accessible as this sort of thing gets.

Machover, M., *Set Theory, Logic and Their Limitations*, Cambridge University Press (1996). A well-regarded, advanced textbook.

Tomassi, P., *Logic*, Routledge (1999). There are hundreds of elementary logic textbooks, this is one of the best.

Index